MADE IN AFRICA, MADE IT IN AMERICA

*Dreams come true in America
for a determined African woman*

George Acquaah

Published in the United States of America

ISBN 978-1-953904-59-1 (SC)
ISBN 978-1-956741-89-6 (HC)
ISBN 978-1-955243-26-1 (Ebook)

George Acquaah Publishing
21 Brigadier Ct,
Gettysburg, PN 17325
www.stellarliterary.com

Ordering Information and Rights Permission:

Quantity sales. Special discounts might be available on quantity purchases by corporations, associations, and others. For details, contact the publisher at the address above.

For Book Rights Adaptation and other Rights Permission. Call us at toll free 1- 888-945-8513 or send us email at admin@stellarliteray.com.

ACKNOWLEDGEMENTS

The author acknowledges with thanks and deepest appreciation, the contributions of several people who took the time to review the manuscript at various stages of its preparation, and provided valuable input. First, and most importantly, Theresa, the subject of this book, reviewed it for accuracy of the information. I thank her profoundly for granting me the opportunity to write so candidly about her life story, and more importantly for being a part of it as her husband.

Another family member, Dr. Aaron Barkoh, reviewed the manuscript in its early stages to corroborate the various accounts of the story from the family perspective. I thank him for his support and encouragement throughout the project. Next, I extend special thanks and appreciation to two professional colleagues at Bowie State University, for reviewing the manuscript. Dr. Brenda DoHarris focused on ensuring that my thoughts were expressed properly and clearly. Dr. Monifa Love particularly provided assistance with reorganizing the narrative to flow more logically, be more informative, and sustain the attention of the reader.

Posthumously, I thank Theresa's mother, Madame Isabella Mensah, and grandmother, Madame Eboye Tennachie, who were mostly responsible for her "making," genetically, as well as nurturing her into an adult in Ghana, Africa, prior to going to America. I am very proud to dedicate this book to these wonderful women in Theresa's life.

No one is an island, and no one succeeds alone. Theresa's life is what it is because she had support from family and friends along the way. To all these people, I say a big thank you to you for your kindness and support. Finally, I thank God for blessing me with Theresa as my wife, and affording me the unique opportunity to be part of her unfolding.

CONTENTS

DEDICATION

To Madame Isabella Mensah and Madame Eboyie Tennachie

Chapter 1

The Model Wife

am a plant scientist and I have devoted my life to studying how plants grow and thrive. I understand the genetics of plants, how they interact with their environment, and how they can be improved so they perform better. I have written several academic textbooks about plants, so it is then no wonder that I have considered writing a biography about my wife, beautiful flower that she is. I believe her life story is too compelling, inspiring, challenging and remarkable to remain untold. My quandary has been how to tell the story of someone to whom I am yoked. As her husband of over 35 years, I have had a front row seat to my wife's unfolding, and I have played some role in her flowering, so I pray. Some book projects flow rather smoothly from conception to completion; others are start-stop-go because something does not "click" for me. This book is a case in point for the latter scenario. That is, until one blessed summer day. It was Friday, August 15, 2013. Theresa called to tell me that she had shared a letter I had written about her with a friend. I wrote the letter over a decade ago to *The Oprah Winfrey Show*. At that time, the *Show* invited viewers to nominate people to be considered for a surprise treat by the legendary celebrity, Oprah. The goal of the segment was to celebrate people who were so dedicated to the service of others that they neglected themselves. If selected, the *Oprah Show* did what Oprah is known to do best - celebrate life, and the lucky person was pampered like a queen or king, Oprah style.

My beloved wife and I were living in Oklahoma when I wrote the letter. More on our unusual Oklahoma circumstances later. I did it without her knowledge and input, since it was meant to be a surprise. I thought my wife was the embodiment of such a personality. And so, I penned, in a matter of minutes, a letter that was from the heart. It was a sincere, unapologetic, and unashamed praise poem for my soulmate. If you had what I have, you'd be poetic, too. Including the letter will give the whole storyline away, and so I have decided against doing that. In fact, I considered tucking it away somewhere in the back, but thought some readers might "cheat" and read it right away and thereby ruin the surprise. In the letter, I described my wife's many wonderful attributes with the hopes that Oprah would recognize her with some lavish prize. Although the letter did not bring her the acclaim I had hoped, it meant a lot to Theresa. From 2003 to 2013, she had shared the letter with friends and family members all over the globe, and she read it every now and then, getting emotional about it every time. At the end of our conversation, I asked her to email a copy to me. It arrived about thirty seconds later. It pleased me that it was something she had readily available. I recollected as much of the letter as my "male brain" allowed me to, but there were details I had not remembered, and as I read it through I knew immediately that it would be the basis of the book about my wife that I had been contemplating for years.

My wife's talents and personal philosophy in life were formed in Africa, specifically, Ghana, our homeland. It is her Ghanaian upbringing that nurtured those talents and skills as a life partner. Theresa was born and raised, and literally made in Africa. It is the value system she acquired there that helped her to effectively and successfully navigate the challenges and access the opportunities offered her in order to make it in America. Hence, the title of this book: "Made in Africa, Made it in America" is designed to recognize how Theresa's life has been shaped by both cultures. Of course, the narrative will have to be in the context of married life and include, especially, her husband's influence, since the two are one in marriage and both lived together in America. Nonetheless, I have made every effort to shine the spot light most brightly on her, and less on the supporting cast of spouse, family members, friends, and children.

It is my intention to make this book accessible to everyone. However, Theresa and I are who and what we are because of our Christian faith. Consequently, it is impossible to completely mute what is an integral part of our being and lifestyle. Also, although we are citizens of the United States of America, our roots are in Ghana. Ghana has changed significantly over the past thirty-seven years and more since Theresa and I left our beloved country for America. Some readers, especially those from Ghana, and more especially those who are much younger and did not know the Ghana (or Gold Coast) in which we grew up, may find conditions that I reference to have passed away. Some might even be disappointed and wonder why I am harping on the past, when Ghana today is so different in many ways. Nonetheless, it is these conditions and values that provide the foundation for Theresa's approach to life and to our tremendous adventure as husband and wife. Telling it any other way will make the story less authentic and relevant. We are as proud of our country's past as we are of its present, and hope that we can contribute to make the future even more glorious. When necessary, I shall indicate to readers the status of the conditions in the country as at writing, but not to the extent that it takes away from Theresa's conduct and experiences, and thereby minimize her stellar accomplishments.

When I told Theresa that I would be using the letter as a point of departure for the book, she pointed out a minor misstatement of fact in the draft (women!). This indicates how accurately she wants her story to be told. In my exuberance and excitement, I had stated that her Chrysler minivan had over 300,000 miles on the odometer. It was only about 200,000 miles. She wanted to be accurate and not appear to extenuate her circumstances, but later on, one of her cars, an Oldsmobile, "lived" to be more than 300,000 miles! Also, there are a few typos and a "major" misstatement of fact in the letter - our wedding date (men!), but the letter is one of the most important tokens of our marriage. I am not sure about the fate of the Oprah letter. I don't know how far up in the review process it got, or if it was ever read by anyone at all. But I am very happy that Theresa appreciated it, and that she continues to cherish it, and that is priceless.

Before I share with you the attributes of my African Queen, let me pose this question to the reader. If you are an unmarried man, what do you hope for in a *perfect* wife? If you are married, what do you expect from your wife? Is a perfect wife born or made? I took time to research the answers to these and related questions about perfection in one's spouse. I share some of the key attributes that many expect in an ideal wife in the following paragraphs.

Certain attributes attract us to the opposite sex and make us fall in love. A physically beautiful woman or handsome man is always a "looker" who turns heads and is highly desired. For some, physical attraction or anatomical features are very high on their list of desirable qualities in a mate. These include a certain desired height and weight, skin color or tone, color of eyes, size and shape of facial features, hair color, to name just a few traits. Some like tall and slim women, while others prefer women with "some meat on the bones." A combination of these traits conjures up an image that makes many men pause and say: "Wow, she is a beautiful woman," or "She is a sexy lady." Thanks to advances in technology and in medical science, changes in anatomical features are only a scalpel away. Some women do not hesitate to go under the knife for minor and sometimes even major cosmetic makeovers.

Is outward beauty all that counts, if I may ask? Absolutely not. Inner beauty is priceless. Society acknowledges such a thing as "love at first sight." Much of this emotion or feeling is triggered by physical appearance or outward beauty. Put another way, we tend to "judge the book by its cover," when we meet people for the first time. Looks may cause one to lock eyes with someone at first sight, but it takes inner beauty, the expression of the soul, to create an attraction. Is beauty really in the eye of the beholder? What is beautiful to one may not be so to another. However, it can be argued that inner beauty, for example, an expression of compassion or kindness, can be beheld by anyone. Outward beauty may hook and reel one in, but inner beauty is what keeps the catch. Outer beauty, they say, is skin deep. It can be groomed and dressed up, but as another popular axiom goes, "Clothes do not make the man."

Character is important in a marriage and life in general. A good wife should have integrity and be trustworthy. She should be industrious. Theresa's life was shaped by two women, her mother and paternal grandmother. One might say of these women that when, sometime in their existence life threw them a curve ball, they did not strike out. They forged on ahead with determination, and made sacrifices to achieve their dreams. The apple does not fall far from the tree, they say. Theresa's life story as told in this book mirrors that of these mentors. More will be said about them later.

We get ideas about the desirable spouse from our experiences, especially, watching our parents or relatives, as well as other people live out the married life. We get ideas also from reading books on the subject or attending workshops and seminars on relationship and marriage. We all hope to find our prince or princess charming, and marry and live happily ever after. The reality, as they say, is that marriages are made in heaven, but they are lived on earth. Obviously, is it impossible to enumerate all the attributes of a desirable or perfect wife. Some attributes are more important to some men than others. One of my favorite guides to the qualities of a perfect wife is found in the Bible (Proverbs 31: 10- 31).

Many women do noble things, but Theresa surpasses them all! A modern wife can be industrious and manage her home with diligence. She plans ahead to ensure that her family is taken care of. She plans for the seasonal needs of her children in terms of clothes, and as "Soccer Mom," has the honor of driving the children to a myriad of afterschool activities - soccer practice, band, piano, swimming, dance, church programs, to name a few. A modern wife may have to work a fulltime job, and sometimes is the breadwinner of the house, while the man does the honors as "Mr. Mom." She may be better at managing the finances of the home than her husband. "A wife of noble character who can find?" inquires the Bible. Well, I believe I have been blessed with such a one! Come along with me on this journey while I substantiate my claim.

5

Chapter 2

The African Woman

Theresa arrived in America as a brand new wife to start the next phase of her life as a family woman, an African woman in America. It is important that her story be told from the perspective of how an African woman, a wife, survived and thrived in America as a mother, student, and professional. The narrative in this chapter is also critical to appreciating the sacrifices that Theresa had to make, and the privileges she had to forfeit, in order to make it in America.

One's environment, culture, and upbringing significantly impact one's value system and lifestyle. Theresa was raised in keeping with West African culture, specifically, Ghanaian culture. This will be discussed in much detail in the subsequent chapters. By the time she was transplanted into the Western culture, after college in Ghana, she had already been molded by the value system of her native culture. One may ask, "Can an old dog be taught new tricks?" Well, it depends. Some traditional values cannot and must not be compromised; others may be revised in the light of situations in one's new environment. In this story, the reader would see how an African woman used the skills she had gained through her upbringing to successfully navigate the complexities of contemporary American society.

When I say that Theresa is an African woman, what do I mean? Is there such a thing as a *typical* African woman? Who is she? Unlike

America, a country, and relatively homogeneous one at that, Africa is a continent that comprises of over fifty countries. An "African woman" may be too broad a generalization to describe. Many of us resent it when Africa is spoken of as if it were a homogeneous country like the US. The typical African woman has been portrayed in both positive and negative light in various media around the globe, sometimes by people who only watch her from afar as an object of curiosity. The reality is that, African women exist and operate across the full spectrum of lifestyles, from the very rural and traditional (agrarian) to the sophisticated and ultramodern (high-tech or upper class). This notwithstanding, the reference to "the typical African woman" has some merit, largely because some traditional values are hard to abandon, no matter how Westernized or modernized one becomes. In rural areas, which remain steeped in culture and tradition, the African woman is often conservative and modest in her ways. As one moves into the cities and urban areas, where people are exposed to and interact more intimately with the global community, the African woman tends to be more liberal and cosmopolitan.

Anatomically, some of the most beautiful women in the world are found in Africa. African beauties have and continue to flaunt "their stuff" on some of the world's most prestigious runways, as models and super models. Generally, African cultures celebrate plumpness rather than the thinness that is promoted in Western cultures. The typical African woman is more generously endowed in the front and back anatomical areas, bosoms and buttocks to be precise. She wants to have children, not just one or two, but several.

Theresa wanted six! Having children is high priority in a marriage in Africa. It does not matter whether one is a professional or not, as a married woman, sooner or later, one would be expected to have children.

The African woman is industrious and very hard working. She plays a significant role in the socioeconomics of her country. She is family-oriented and very devoted to her children's wellbeing. She is not afraid to get her hands dirty. She will do whatever it takes to put food on the table for the family and keep clothes on their backs. In rural areas, women are actively engaged on family farms. In the towns and cities, their outstanding entrepreneurial acumen drives them into trading and all kinds of small business enterprises.

One characteristic about the African culture is hospitality. We open our homes to strangers and take care of them. Women play a significant role in this by being good hostesses. A wife is expected to be a good cook. A critical difference between Western and African women in the culinary area is that, the latter do not use "cheat sheets" as guide. They generally do not cook from recipe books – no precise measuring and weighing devices, thermometers, food processors, etc. But they can cook a myriad of dishes all from memory, and consistently deliver identical outcomes each time. Traditionally, the man as the head of the family, provides money for food for the household (called chop money). A woman without planning and managerial skills often overspends the budget.

With education, the modern African woman has become even more empowered to excel to reach new horizons. But no matter how "Westernized" she becomes, a typical African woman never abandons certain basic cultural values, as previously indicated. When overseas, she is very well served by such cultural attributes. In college in the US, I observed clear distinctions between African women and women from other parts of the world. Many African women on campus had accompanied their husbands who were pursuing higher degrees in their fields in the US. Whereas many women from other cultures limited themselves mostly to taking care of the home, many African women often combined such housekeeping tasks withembarking on higher education themselves. Others engaged in all kinds of odd jobs and small businesses to help support the family. If the men were on scholarships or fellowships, the stipends were seldom adequate to support a wife, let alone raising a family, which was often the case. African women are very polite and respectful, behavior that sometimes can be misconstrued by those in the West as being subservient to their husbands. It is fair to say that the traditional roles of women as homemakers, in charge of housekeeping, and even waiting on men to some extent, linger in some modern African homes. However, as the reality of a two-income family sinks in, many progressive men are willing to chip in to support women in doing "a woman's job." Many African women are religious. They believe in God as creator and sustainer of life. They are also political to some extent. While overseas, they immerse themselves in the culture of their host country, as much as is necessary to survive and thrive. They learn to juggle family, education and career.

As African women increasingly pursue professional careers and enter the workforce at rates comparable to those of men, the two partners in a marriage tend to depend on and support each other more than previously. In fact, African women are increasingly assuming leadership roles in business, government and the corporate world. They have to juggle career with raising a family, something that requires some support from the husband to be successful.

In the West, daycare for children is a well-established industry. It is relatively easier for the working woman to drop off her child at a professional daycare center on the way to work and pick him or her up after work. These services are not common back home in Ghana. On the other hand, it is very common for a professional woman to have a maid at home to do the chores and help with preparing food for the family. If a professional woman in Ghana has a new baby, it is common for a family member, usually her mother, to come to live with her for several months, to help with housekeeping and childcare. Mothers are revered and respected in the traditional context. Insulting another's mother is not a wise thing to do, as it could end you in hot waters. As a popular adage goes, "You don't point to your mother's house with your left finger". You see, the left hand is deemed the "lesser hand" in Ghana and is relegated to performing dirt jobs (e.g., picking up trash, cleaning up after a bowel movement, etc.). Consequently, it is a big no-no to extend you left hand to receive or offer a handshake, or give or receive something from another, especially, an older person. In spite of such a positive and much needed role played by mothers in the homes of their adult children, mothers- in-law are seldom spoken of favorably in Ghana, and I guess in most if not all cultures.

America is a land of opportunity; the world is told. And so many Africans come over to avail themselves of opportunity, just like all other immigrants to the country. That said, east or west, there is no place like home. We all look forward to helping our parents and other family members whom we left behind to pursue opportunity overseas. The African woman overseas works hard for her children in the Diaspora, but also plans for returning home someday. In the meantime, she supports those whom she left behind with regular or periodic remittance.

To sum it up, I believe the African woman has it all, wants it all, and can do it all. The African woman is the ultimate multi-tasker. She can chew gum and walk at the same time, so to speak. The modern African woman may be defined by qualities that transcend cultures and nations. She is proud of her heritage, but is also open to and willing to embrace new opportunities and ideas from other cultures. She is family-oriented, confident, progressive, industrious, capable, and exhibits strong leadership acumen at home, the workplace, and in society in general. The African woman is a force to be reckoned with.

Chapter 3

The Molding

On the shore of the Atlantic Ocean, in the Western Region of Ghana, West Africa, is located the medium-sized town of Esiama, a fishing community that is gradually diversifying and modernizing its economic base. This is where the journey begins for Theresa, nee Abenlema Yankey. Esiama is only about 5 miles from Kikam, another town that features prominently in Theresa's childhood. To get to Esiama, one must cross the mighty Ankobra River. The closest major city is Axim, but closer yet is perhaps the most famous town in the region, and arguably in the country, Nkroful, the birthplace of Dr. Kwame Nkrumah, the founding prime minister of independent Ghana. The native language of the people in that area is Nzema. As a coastal town Esiama enjoys the soothing sea breeze in the afternoon and nighttime. The expansive shore line provides opportunities for a leisurely stroll along the beach and a dip in the sea, if one is so inclined. The family home was close to the beach, but grandma's home, where Theresa was raised, was farther into the town.

Commercially, the sea provides a livelihood for the people as a source of fresh fish and other sea food. Theresa fondly recalls the times when she and others went to assist fishermen to drag in their nets, partly for adventure and fun, but also for rewards of a few fish thrown their way every now and then. My favorite reason for desiring to live by the sea is fresh coconut, and Esiama has lots of it along its coastline. When I visited my in-laws for the first time, a request was promptly placed to harvest a basket full of the delicious nuts for my enjoyment. Mature and dry coconuts are processed into coconut oil.

Commercial mills operate alongside local cottage industries to produce and market this flavorful oil.

Every town has its culture and festivals. Esiama has *Kundum*, a festival to give thanks to God for a good harvest. It brings together townsfolk from far and near for family reunions. The celebration starts on a Sunday, and goes on for eight days. The key activities are drumming, dancing and feasting. A highlight of the festival is the pageantry that involves a procession through the streets of the town, with the chief aloft in his palanquin on the shoulders of strong young men. Participants usually dress up in distinctive *Kundum* attires and footwear, sometimes accessorizing with decorative masks. Traditionally, visits are paid to shrines at the outskirts of the town. Libation is poured along with animal sacrifices in the stool room of the palace. Ritual dances are performed as the festival is also one for expelling demons and evil spirits from the town. The townsfolk are selective as to the manner in which they celebrate the event and the activities in which they choose to participate. Christians usually stay away from the pagan rituals. Theresa fondly recalls especially the family reunions over the past years that the festival afforded. Siblings from overseas and all over the country gather to reminisce.

The importance of early childhood training in life cannot be overemphasized. Proverbs 22:6 states: "Train a child in the way he should go; even when he is old he will not depart from it." Theresa's upbringing is pivotal to her success in adulthood as a student, wife, mother and professional. Let me start with this sobering statement of fact. There may not have been a story to tell, and this book would not have been needed, if Theresa had been born in a village and to parents without means. While writing this book, Theresa remarked one evening to my astonishment: "Had I been born in a village, I might not have been here today," she said. I asked why, and that is when she explained that she was born premature, and might not have survived childbirth. After that exchange, I appreciated even the more her strong desire to return home to help address feminine health issues. The reality of village life, especially in those days, is that modern healthcare services are nonexistent or scarce at best. Prenatal care is not part of the lives of most pregnant women, especially in rural areas of

Africa. Child delivery is done primarily by midwives and sometimes by an experienced older woman in town, who has no formal training in midwifery. Consequently, complications at childbirth could result in the death of both mother and child, as there is no means to readily transport patients to well-equipped and better staffed hospitals in distant cities.

Babies who are born very premature are almost certain to face death, especially those with severe abnormalities. Even with the intervention of a midwife, a child who has severe respiratory challenges at birth is not likely to live long thereafter. As described later in the book, our first two children were born premature, but are now healthy and thriving adults, because they were born in the USA. They spent weeks in intensive care, their vital signs constantly monitored by sophisticated equipment and highly trained medical staff.

Being born to the late Madame Bozuma Miezah and the late Mr. Paul Yankey, then Assistant Police Commissioner and Director of Research Department (Annex) of the Ministry of Foreign Affairs, and Personal Assistant to Dr. Kwame Nkrumah, the founding Prime Minister of the Republic of Ghana, would suggest a life of privilege for Theresa. Not quite so. She never really knew her father, who died when she was only about three years. He died at the tender age of forty-four years, while returning home from accompanying Dr. Nkrumah on an official trip to Casablanca, Morocco. The story is that his flight arrived late in the evening. Mr. Yankey was eager to attend his uncle's funeral and therefore insisted on travelling straight on to Esiama, several hours away. At some point on the way, he insisted on driving the car himself and relieved the driver of his duties. Shortly after they traded places, he ran into a stationary truck and was killed instantly.

Mr. Yankey had three wives, one from Northern Ghana, and two from the Western Region. Theresa's mother, Madame Bozuma Mensah, was wife number two. Naturally, he had a large family, 14 children in all. Older sister Paulina recalls that their father was a very loving family man. They missed him a lot for he travelled rather frequently. His return home was always met with great expectation from the children, for better and for worse. For better, he always brought beautiful city clothes and goodies for his children. On the worse side, Mr. Yankey was a disciplinarian who did not spare the rod to keep his children on the "straight and narrow." On that fateful day, Paulina recalls that whereas they were eagerly expecting their father back home from Casablanca, there was some trepidation, for they expected to be whipped upon his return for various misdemeanors committed in his absence. Unfortunately, untimely death beat him to it. Mr. Yankey was very proud of his children and wanted and expected them to be successful students and citizens. He did not shy away from bragging about their accomplishments to his friends. Mr. Yankey would have been especially thrilled and proud to see his daughter, Theresa, grow up to be an accomplished professional, as I describe later in the book.

Soon after his passing, his wives and all the children relocated from Accra, the capital city, to Esiama, to be under the matriarchal supervision of grandma Eboyie Tennachie, Theresa's paternal grandmother. The older siblings were dispatched to boarding schools, while Theresa and Agnes, her half-sister, were left at home to assist their grandma. Theresa was raised by her grandmother and her mother. Being born Isabella Yaba Bozuma Mensah, Theresa's mother had a vibrant life of her own. She was previously married to Mr. Bonsu Abban with whom she had a son, David Abban. David was dearly beloved by all. His untimely death at the young age of sixty years, thus preceding his mother in death, was too much for the family to bear. Auntie Isabella, as this popular woman was affectionately called by those who knew her, started life as an elementary school teacher at Nyakrom and Kikam in the Western Region. Mr. Paul Yankey, as the story goes, had gone on a philanthropic mission to Kikam School to donate educational materials, when a pretty young lady, Isabella, caught his eyes. What a catch it was. You might say it pays to be philanthropic. They would soon be married and blessed with five children.

Madam Mensah was widowed at the young age of thirty-three, but remarried later to Mr. Alex Archer with whom she had her last child, Grace. She devoted most of her adult life to raising her children, with the support of Nana Tennachie. When the children were old enough to be independent, she decided to return to work as a receptionist for about seven years before entering the world of business, to raise additional resources to support the college education of her children. Theresa recalled a conversation she overheard one early morning. Her mother and another family member were chatting when the latter expressed concerned about how Auntie Isabella was overextending herself to support the family. That morning, she had woken up with body aches, apparently symptoms of flu. Nonetheless, she was determined not to miss the biggest market day of the week, an opportunity to make good sales from her cloth trading enterprise. Consequently, she responded to that family member, Auntie Dorothy, this way: "It is all for the children. If I don't do it, who will? School will soon reopen. They'll need their supplies for school. I have to make some money to meet the expenses." The apple does not fall far from the tree, they say. Theresa is a chip off the old block in terms of the sacrifices she makes for the sake of her family's wellbeing and success.

Because of Mr. Paul Yankey's stature, the family was very prominent and highly regarded in town. Their living conditions were relatively very good. Even in those days, they had running water and indoor plumbing, as well as a private generator for electricity, which was not the case for most people in town. Of course, in every country, there are the "haves" and "have-nots." Children of privilege often live in homes with maids and houseboys to do the household chores. Unfortunately, this was not Theresa's experience. Grandma Tennachie had no formal education but she was determined to provide it for her grandchildren. She was a staunch Roman Catholic. Even though Theresa's lot was very favorable, she was not raised as a spoiled brat. Every morning, the cock crowed with the precision of a Swiss watch to herald the dawn of another day. "What will the day be like?" Theresa would wonder. In Ghana, and especially in the "good old days," children had daily chores they had to perform with religious fervor, no ifs ands or buts. The advantage of doing chores is that children grow up to be more responsible, with good work ethics

and excellent survival, social and housekeeping skills. They tend to be more resilient, hardworking, and well-mannered.

Children in Ghana are trained to be very respectful of their elders. In addition to speaking sternly to children, spanking is always a ready option for use for disciplining wayward kids. Theresa generally managed to stay out of trouble, but even she could not escape the rod. She recalls the most severe whipping she ever received, that came at the hand of grandma. The family house was huge, with rooms to accommodate all the children and others when they reunited on vacations. During those days, the house chores were several times more intense. She recalls having three wooden mortars simultaneously in operation, in order to prepare the favorite traditional dish, *fufu*, to feed the large group of people. The children took turns to pound the plantain and cassava into a sticky paste, a very tiring chore. Theresa had completed a turn at one of the pounding stations and was taking a much needed and deserved break. As grandma passed by, older sister Paulina decided it was time to have some fun by getting baby sister into trouble. Well, she picked the wrong time to do so. She instructed Theresa in grandma's hearing to interrupt her break to assist her, knowing full well that Theresa had just completed a turn at a pounding station. Afraid of grandma's wrath, she promptly cut short her break and proceeded to assist Paulina. That was when big sister decided to enjoy her "victory" by teasing and making funny faces at her sister. But before she had time to savor her ill- gotten victory, Theresa responded immediately with a spectacular slap across Paulina's face. Of course, grandma heard it all and turned around to investigate. That was when all hell broke loose on Theresa's butt. She had a life changing epiphany that day.

Grandma had a front-house mom-and-pop store. It was Theresa's daily chore to open it early in the morning and ready it for business, and then pack things up and close the shop in the evening. Other chores included sweeping the large compound and rooms in the house, assisting with cooking, and cleaning dishes after meals. Even during the lunch break, Theresa had to run home from school to assist with preparing lunch. As such, she was perpetually late for school. Later on in life, Theresa's store experience would come in handy, as she developed into a shrewd shopper. Chores were more intense on weekends. Additional activities included more thorough cleaning of the bedrooms and living rooms, going to the market to buy food for the week, doing the laundry – hers and grandma's – by hand (no washing machines were available then), and other duties. Sometimes, grandma woke her up in the morning to go to the backyard garden to do some weeding, before returning to her daily house chores. She recalls even going to fetch firewood from the bush for the house on some weekends. These chores provided opportunities for her to learn and hone her organizational and planning skills. Sunday was church time. Children and adults donned their Sunday best. There were no Wendy's or McDonald's restaurants in those days, or eating out after church, but often the Sunday lunch was special.

The educational system in Ghana was initially structured after the British system. Significant modifications continue to be made after independence on March 6th, 1957. The general progressive stages in education originally were from primary school, to middle school, to secondary school, and then to university. Of course, one could exit at various stages and for various reasons, to attend a trade or technical school, or go to training college. With time, the education system has been overhauled and tweaked under various administrations. Depending on the size of the community, a town may have both primary and middle schools. Otherwise, students have to walk, sometimes several miles, to another town to attend school. Getting to school in those days was the student's responsibility. There were no school buses. And yes, there were chores at school as well. There were no professional janitors or groundskeepers on hand. Chores included sweeping the school yard, cleaning the classrooms, mowing the lawn by cutlass (machete) - no lawn mowers. Unfortunately, one could not file a complaint against the teacher or school for punishing one's child. There were no PTOs (parent teacher organizations).

School started with the morning assembly of all pupils in the open courtyard. They sang the national anthem, recited the pledge of allegiance, sang a hymn, prayed, listened to announcements and then marched into their various classrooms. In Theresa's days, there were

17

no computers or other electronic classroom technology. Part of the school supply list in the primary school was a black wooden slate and a box of white chalk. Notebooks and exercise books were used later on in the education system. There were morning classroom drills, called "'mental." For example, pupils had to memorize the multiplication tables at grade-appropriate level, and were also expected to solve mathematical problems mentally. At school, Theresa worked very hard and loved all subjects, even though mathematics appeared to be her favorite subject. She was noted as an excellent student at her Methodist Elementary School. Her blue uniform, trimmed in yellow with a matching yellow belt, the traditional colors of the Methodist Church, was always neat and well pressed. She had friends at school, but did not have the luxury of "hanging out" with them after school. There just was no time for that kind of after school lifestyle. The extensive chores at home left little room for focusing on academics, yet she was always among the top performers in her class. Theresa learned some of her money management skills early in life. She saved most of her lunch money.

Upon returning home from school, Theresa's evening chores started in earnest - cooking, cleaning, manning the store, etc. She had to complete all chores before settling down to do homework. She had to man her grandma's store until 9.00 pm each night. She wonders how she excelled at school despite all these demanding chores. Thank God she had electric light to help her do her work. Most of the children in town had to make do with kerosene lanterns or lamps as the primary source of light in the night. Coming from a home where children were properly disciplined and taught good manners, Theresa seldom got into trouble at school. Theresa's older siblings were all in boarding schools, attending preparatory school and high school. Consequently, during the holidays, they returned to the family home for a family reunion of sort. Those were times when high school students compared notes and traded high school war and fish stories, as well as new dance moves, to the admiration and envy of those who were left behind in the small town. There was nothing but sibling love and support in the Yankey house; no rivalries that Theresa can recall.

Whereas primary and middle school education were nonresidential, secondary schools in those days were almost entirely residential or boarding, and were located in various regions of the country. One could travel hundreds of miles to a high school in another region of the country and be gone for months. Boarding school education is one of the most cherished and valuable experiences in our educational system in Ghana. By being away from parents, students learn independence and responsibility. One lives in a dorm, shares communal bath rooms, does laundry by hand, makes his or her own bed, goes to the dining room promptly or be without a meal, and attends class on time. Observing siesta, lights out, curfew, and other restrictions, are all part of boarding school experience. There are regular dorm inspections, and students who step out of line are promptly and appropriately disciplined. All boarding schools, and in fact schools in general, have prescribed school uniforms, and sometimes even shoes. To be spared the ordeal of eating the universally-dreaded "school food," families may visit their children over the weekend and bring them home-cooked food.

When it was time, Theresa attended the Mfantsiman Girls High School, one of the prestigious schools in the country. As a young girl, Theresa had a very volatile temper, as described in the previous chapter in the slapping incidence with her older sister. Before she left home for high school, her grandmother and mother sat her down one dawn and gave her a stern lecture, cautioning her about the need to manage her temper, and to make the best use of the opportunity to get an education. The advice happened to be just what the doctor ordered, for in high school, her temper would be tested. One day a school bully started to yank her chain, as they say, teasing and taunting her every step of the way. Naturally, she was tempted to pounce on this girl and beat the tar out of her. Then, she recalled her grandmother's admonition to keep her temper under control. She turned the other cheek and walked away. A short while later, the girl whom she forgave came down with a violent life-threatening illness. If she had followed through and beaten her up, she could have been falsely blamed for causing that episode of ill-health. Her high school was only about a thirty- minute drive from Cape Coast town where she spent some of her holidays with her auntie, Dorothy, a superb cook. She regularly cooked delicious foods and sent them over to her niece. After high school, Theresa attended the University of Cape Coast (UCC), where she studied for a BSc, Agricultural Science degree, with a diploma in Education. What led to this choice will be described in detail in the next chapter.

Unfortunately, grandma Tennachie died during the first year that Theresa entered college. She did not have the pleasure of seeing the fruits of her labors - her granddaughter becoming a successful wife, mother and professional. Theresa owes much of her qualities as a person and professional to the outstanding upbringing of her grandmother and her mother. The experiences gained from this upbringing would come in handy later in the US, as Theresa pursued a career and family life. I asked Theresa to sum up for me the lessons she learned from being in the care of her grandmother. She first cited her strong personality. She had two children, one of whom she lost at a very early age. She was left with an only child, Theresa's father, who died tragically in his early forties. Notwithstanding this and other adversities, she went on to raise fourteen grandchildren. She was industrious, dabbling in various business enterprises to raise funds for the family. She had great organizational skills. Grandma was caring and family- oriented, always ensuring that everyone had what was needed. Is it any wonder that her granddaughter, Theresa, would grow up to embody these excellent qualities?

Chapter 4

The Dream

hildren are often asked this age-old question: "What do you hope to be when you grow up?" The answer a child gives is usually shaped by what he or she is exposed to in society, through parental example at home or in the extended family, programs on TV, information from books, play toys, among others. Often a child wants to be like a hero in the community, someone helpful to people, a celebrity, or a highly respected person. Children in the West often long to be a police officer, entertainer, firefighter, teacher, doctor, or athlete. For many youths, money is the least consideration in career choice. Children are enamored with these professions because they are visible in the community. Some of these professionals, such as doctors and teachers, are directly involved in the lives of children. Some professions are popularized by the toy industry that celebrates them by depicting them in toys and action figures for children to play with. Examples are paramedic, doctor, astronaut, and vehicles like ambulance, fire truck, and police car.

In Africa, toys are usually not part of growing up for most children, except the privileged. Children are very creative, designing play things with whatever junk they can find. Theresa had a fair amount of toys to play with as a child. She also enjoyed simple traditional games such as hop scotch and *ampe*, a very popular game for girls, which is similar to playing "rock paper scissors", only this time it is played with the legs. Yes, we also think that playing football with the hands is strange.

Doctors are not visible in the lives of most children in Ghana, in the way it is in America, since regular visits to the doctor are not part of the lives of most children or even most adults. One sees the doctor only when one is sick. How can a child dream about becoming an engineer, a fireman, doctor, lawyer, astronaut, or any of the traditionally glamorous professions, when he or she knows very little about them? It is disheartening to watch exceptionally talented children drop out of school, just because their parents could not afford to support them, or because the parents needed them to assist on the farm or at home. For many, the dream ends after middle school education, when parents have to finance their children's education on their own. Many are unable to afford the fees to support their children in boarding school in the cities, where the secondary schools are located.

I have already indicated that Theresa comes from a reasonably well to do family. Growing up, Theresa had access to information and influential people to help broaden her horizon and help her to dream about the future. However, her dreams and aspirations were grounded in her observation of the plight of the people in her town and surrounding areas. While she had access to decent health services, she watched other children suffer and sometimes even die from preventable diseases. More troubling for her was the plight of women. Some lost their children during childbirth, while some even died in the process, all stemming from inadequatem health services. The privileged, who can afford it, may access high quality private health care. The situation is dire in the rural areas, where people resort to herbal medicines and visits to the native doctor for all health needs. Prenatal care for pregnant women is unavailable to most women, contributing to various complications associated with childbirth and infant health. As previously stated, child delivery in rural areas is commonly conducted by persons without sufficient professional training, further jeopardizing the health and safety of women and infants. Ambulance service is poor or nonexistent in rural areas. Major hospitals exist in distant cities and are usually overburdened from the influx of patients from all over the region.

When Theresa reached the high school level, she knew the professional career to pursue would be medicine. She wanted to become a doctor; not because it is such a glamorous profession and one of the most lucrative, but primarily to help alleviate the plight of women in her community. Admittedly, most of the existing challenges in the current healthcare system would require governmental intervention to resolve. The challenges are so daunting that even a little effort from an individual can go a long way. Theresa is determined to make whatever contribution she can, little or big, to help those less fortunate than she is.

Of course one can dream all one wants and have confirmations over and over again. Nothing will happen unless one gives wings to his or her dream. To make her dream come true, Theresa worked very hard in school to get good grades to qualify for medical school. At the time, there were only two medical schools in the country, at the University of Ghana, Legon, and the Kwame Nkrumah University of Science and Technology in Kumasi. It is needless to say that entrance to medical school was extremely competitive. In those days, one went to medical school straight from high school. Of course, the school system in Ghana is structured differently from what obtains in the US. In Theresa's days, one went to high school for seven years before going to college. The options in high school were few, and the academic programs so inflexible. Students were segregated early into a few rigid programs in the first five years: Arts, Pure Science, Agricultural Science, Physics and Mathematics, and a couple of others. The choices were even fewer in the next two years of what was called the Sixth Form. For example, my subject combination was zoology, botany and chemistry (aka, Zoo-Bot-Chem). Theresa's course combinations were biology, chemistry and physics. At the end of the five years of high school, we had to take a regional exam - WAEC (West African Exams Council) GCE (General Certificate of Education) Ordinary Level (or O-Level) exams - to qualify to continue for the Sixth Form. To go to university, one had to take the Advanced Level (or A-Level) exams. Admission to medical school took into account mainly one's performance at the A-Level exams.

Demonstration of proficiency in certain science courses, in addition to certain general requirements, was necessary for Theresa's admission to medical school. Her performance in physics at the A-level was average. In that very highly competitive environment, she could not compete for admission to medical school. With that, the door was almost slammed shut to her dream of going to medical school. There was another path, though, albeit not promising. She could repeat the coursework in hope of getting better grades and then reapply. However, the second chance success rate was low as previous applications were placed in the same pool as the current ones, thus making the competition even much keener.

Even though her dream of going to medical school did not materialize after high school, Theresa was about to experience a greater life changing experience in college. It was at UCC that she met her prince charming! How are marriages conducted in Ghana? Let me state categorically that I don't intend to give a detailed account of courtship and marriage traditions in Ghana, nor am I qualified to do so. Every culture has its own customs of bringing about this union. Some are simple, others are very elaborate. Usually, it is a two-family affair, with varying degrees of parental involvement. A marriage essentially unites two families, hopefully, without family feuds down the line. In some Ghanaian cultures, marriages are arranged, whereby parents seek and negotiate spouses on behalf of their children. In other cultures, especially those in Western societies, the choice is largely left to the couple to make. Parents, of course, have opinions and sometimes even advise their children against advancing a relationship to marriage, if they do not approve of the man or woman. Polygamy is tolerated in certain cultures in Ghana. I stated earlier that Theresa's father had three wives.

So, how did we come together? After my MSc degree at the University of Ghana, I accepted a position as Assistant Lecturer to assist a UNESCO/UNDP team to establish a brand new School of Agriculture at UCC. This was the same year in which Theresa enrolled in the agricultural program. But it was in the fourth year that we struck up a relationship. The next order of business was to inform our parents and seek their blessing. Theresa is from the Western

Region of Ghana, while I come from the Eastern Region - different tribes, different languages and customs, etc. The preference, worldwide I believe, is for one to marry from within his or her tribe. Some traditionalists insist on this custom. However, with modernization and globalization, many progressive families gladly accept inter-tribal marriages. Our families gave their blessing and paved the way for us to tie the knot.

The truth of the matter is that intercultural or intertribal marriages have their challenges. The most significant challenge, perhaps, is language. Even though Theresa and I speak different native languages (Nzema and Guan, respectively), our tribes are quite close enough that we both understand a common secondary language. The Akan group, the largest ethnic group in Ghana, is united by a fundamental language, Twi, of which there are several dialects, the major ones being Ashanti, Fante, and Akwapim. My mother is from the Akwapim tribe of Eastern Ghana. If one can speak any of the three major Akan dialects, one can pretty much be at home anywhere within that ethnic group and the country. English is the official language of communication in Ghana. So, language wise, Theresa and I have no problem communicating as a couple. The problem comes when we are in the company of family members. It is understandable that when we are with family members we would communicate naturally and mostly in our language. It is then our role to ensure that a reasonable balance is maintained during such times, so that the families can enjoy their time together without anyone feeling neglected. As a solution, it is common for one spouse to learn the primary language of the other. I have picked up significant vocabulary to have a working knowledge of Nzema.

Traditional marriage is a relatively simple affair in Ghana. Once the couple has been introduced to the two families and received their blessings, an event that usually involves the giving and receiving of gifts (including alcoholic drinks, etc.), the couple is essentially husband and wife. Knot-tying in Ghana has three general stages - knocking, engagement, and wedding, each of which may be celebrated with its unique pomp and circumstance. These days, things are being streamlined and simplified to reduce the costs of these events. The "knocking fee" if you will, can be as simple as a bottle of liquor, usually a high-end brand, which is presented by the suitor to the woman's parents. This gesture alerts them that he is not only courting their daughter but has the intention to marry her in the near future. Consequently, the parents should not entertain any other offers from other men. The woman's family may request some commitment from the man, by way of asking him about a timeline for the engagement and wedding. The engagement is celebrated by the giving of a ring by the man to the woman. This event may occur about a week or more prior to the wedding day. Some families prefer to replace the knocking stage with a longer engagement time. Once engaged, the couple is customarily married, as already stated. The wedding is literally the icing on the cake. Christians, generally, tend to keep the relationship platonic until after the wedding to consummate the union.

Weddings in Ghana can be simple or very fancy, depending on the means of the couple and their families. The event is usually held in a church and officiated by at least one clergy person. In terms of attire, Western traditions are commonly followed in Ghana. The bride dons a white bridal gown, usually fashioned from silk and/or a lacey fabric. She wears a tiara, pulls a train, and is attended by a bridal court of several ladies (flower girls or bridesmaids). Theresa had all these and some more. Those days, the bridal party was very simple. All dresses worn were custom- made. Today, some weddings in Ghana feature several groomsmen and bridesmaids, clad in rented tuxedos or other clothes in some cases, just as obtains in the US. A key attraction at the reception is the wedding cake. Ghanaian wedding cakes have a distinct texture and flavor from American cakes. The former have lots of currants or raisins and tend to be drier and contain a lot of alcohol. Theresa had a four-tiered cake.

Our wedding was held on July 30th, 1983, in Cape Coast, where I lived and worked. It was a difficult summer for the world.

Shortages of food and fuel were rampant. In fact, we could not even find ingredients to bake our wedding cake and to host the kind of reception we wanted. That was quickly resolved when Theresa's older sister, Paulina came to the rescue. She dispatched her daughter, Jenifer, from London, UK, with suitcases of ingredients for the cake, among other items. Photographic films and wedding programs were provided by Dr. Robert Dadson, aka Uncle Bob, a family friend residing in the US. Auntie Dorothy and her husband supported us in various aspects of the wedding celebration. Pals, including Tim Brew (best man), TVO Lamptey, JT Acquaah, Paa Sammy and Kofi Mensah were great supporters on our special day.

. But as the newlyweds continued to enjoy marital bliss, "bad news" was brewing on the horizon. I had accepted a Fulbright Scholarship to pursue a doctoral degree in Plant Breeding and Genetics at Michigan State University, in the US, and was scheduled to leave Ghana in early August, just about a week after the wedding. The scholarship made provision for one person; Theresa was not permitted to travel along for various reasons cited by the US Embassy. In fact, she could not have travelled with me at that time anyhow since, thanks to student unrests at that time, the universities had been closed by the government. At the time the schools were closed, Theresa had one academic term left to complete her degree program, after which she had to fulfill a one- year national service obligation. So on one early August evening in 1983, amidst tears, we said our goodbyes, before I boarded a plane for a flight to Minneapolis-St Paul, Minnesota, USA, to join a contingent of Fulbright Scholars from all over the world, for a pre- academic program. It would be about a whole year before we would be reunited. What a way to start a marriage! Little did we know at that time that it was only a foretaste of what was to come. I should mention here that Theresa had also been offered a scholarship opportunity to study in the UK upon completion of her degree. She declined the offer so she could complete her National Service and join me in the US, thereafter. Living apart is not pleasant or easy, especially, for newlyweds. Our faith and love for each other would sustain us.

With my arrival in America, the stage was set for another chance for Theresa's "dream" to move to another phase and on course for realization. We tied the knot in Ghana, Africa, where the dream was born. Now, we were heading to America, where we hoped the dream would manifest. I was the advance party to our new country to lay the groundwork for building our new home. Apart from studying, the other major item on my agenda was planning for Theresa to join me. To do so, I had to request a J-2 visa application form the International Students Office on campus. That was not difficult. The US Embassy in Ghana needed evidence that I could support my wife. Then I had to purchase a ticket for her. The latter two were a little more challenging, but I managed to satisfy them. After about a year all by myself, I was more than ready for the reunion!

Chapter 5

The Reunion and our Plan

n chapter four, I stated that I felt I was sent ahead to America to prepare the place for Theresa's arrival. We got married in Ghana. The question now was how we were going to live as a couple in a strange land. Some background information about the road leading to the reunion is worth sharing. Many people in Ghana learn about the US largely through the printed matter and various mass media. Movies show both the good and bad sides of the country, depending on the subject matter. The fancy skylines of American cities and the lifestyles of the rich and famous in Hollywood are always awe-inspiring and attractive to people from challenging circumstances around the world. People are fascinated by millionaires and billionaires; musicians and other performers from America are trend-setters. Whatever is a hit in the US, sooner or later becomes the standard overseas. Theresa and I were no different in our admiration of America, especially, for its high quality educational system. Neither of us had travelled to the US prior to this time. All we knew about the country, we learned at school in geography or world history classes, in addition to what came by way of the news media. Most of the professors with terminal degrees at that time studied overseas, often in the US, Canada or UK. They also provided some information about the country and life there.

After one summer semester at the University of Minnesota, I departed for East Lansing, Michigan, the home of Michigan State University, the Spartans, where I had been assigned to pursue my doctoral studies. Michigan State, like the University of Minnesota, was a huge campus that enrolled over 40,000 students. I settled into my shared apartment in Spartan Village, the residential complex for mostly international students. This was to be my abode for a whole year by myself, while Theresa did likewise in Ghana. This was to be the first of several unplanned separations that would characterize our marriage to date.

Michigan State has one of the largest international programs in the nation. At that time, there was a large contingent of Africans on campus, of which Ghanaians were significantly represented. There were several of my countrymen and countrywomen in my situation - separated from their spouses. Separation at any time is unpleasant, but especially difficult when it occurs only about a week after a wedding. I got down to the business for which I had come to the US in the first place. I hit the books hard. I was also very active in the African Christian Fellowship as well as the International Outreach United (IOU), an organization founded by Rev. Wolf.

Meanwhile, in Ghana, Theresa went about her life without me, the best she could. She enrolled in a commercial college to learn typing. Her mother was on hand to assist and keep her company, preparing her for married life ahead. Finally, the universities were reopened later that year for business. Theresa went back to complete her degree. She returned to campus with a different status, Mrs. Acquaah. Her friends knew about the wedding before school was shut down, so there was no surprise in that regard. Her focus that year was to complete her degree and get ready to move on to join her husband. She also spent the time strengthening her faith in God, participating more in the Christian Fellowship. Of course, the separation was hard on her as well. She did the best to cope with it. When the time came for her to travel, she applied for a visa from the American Embassy in Accra. It took three attempts before she was successful. The one year forced separation was the first major test of our commitment to each other. It took God's grace and help to make it through. We communicated often via phone and through letters. In a way, all by myself, I was able to focus intensely on my academic program with little distraction. That said, I would have traded the experience for Theresa to be around. After about a year of living apart, the day came for Theresa to travel to the US came, and not a second sooner. Yippee!! I readied the apartment, 38D Spartan Village, as best as I could. Everyone in my department knew about the countdown to D-day (or is it A- day?). On her part, Theresa readied herself the best she could for the journey. It was her first trip out of the country, but she was not anxious about flying or the duration of the flight. The first lap took her to Gatwick Airport in London. She arrived with only $20 in her purse. Thanks to big sister Paulina who lives in the UK and who took the time to meet her at the airport, a potential drama was taken out of the transit experience. Theresa had to completely deplane, take custody of her luggage, and then travel by road to another airport, Heathrow, in London, for the second leg to her final destination. Paulina, a pro at traveling in that part of the world, assisted with the transfer process. Meanwhile, big brother George was awaiting his sister at Heathrow, where they had lunch,

before Theresa emplaned for the US.

She arrived in the US, at the Detroit International Airport, in the night. Without a car of my own at that time, I solicited the assistance of a friend to drive me to the Detroit airport to collect my wife on August 9th, 1984. What a day it was!! My first impression was that Theresa had not changed much. She was as beautiful as ever. She was still her slender self. She arrived clad in typical Ghanaian attire, holding a piece of local artwork. I brought a bouquet of flowers to welcome her. We embraced and shared a kiss, and loaded up for the two-hour trip back to East Lansing, Michigan. Africans, in general, do not display overt affection publicly, but I was learning the American culture and pretty fast. It was late in the night. There was no welcoming party at the apartment. Frankly, it was better that way. After about a year apart, I was lit up like a Christmas tree at the Rockefeller Plaza in New York in December. We needed to rediscover each other and catch up with news, first hand. Theresa thought I had not changed at all, still my slim self. The following day, I introduced her to some close friends in the neighborhood. Pastor and Mrs. Wolf came by to pick us up for church on the first Sunday. Later on, I arranged a welcome reception at home for her to meet my academic team, comprising of my major advisor, Dr. Wayne Adams and Dr. Jim Kelly, another advisor. During the early days of her arrival in the US, we went around town on several occasions, so she could get a feel for how an American city looked like.

I wish we could have had the time to have the real honeymoon we did not have after our wedding. Unfortunately, when Theresa arrived, I was knee deep in my doctoral program. I regret that I could not just suspend my work for several weeks to relax with her as much as she needed. Some of the things we had only read about or seen in movies and heard on newscasts were now being played out in real time. The good, the bad and the ugly were unfolding right before our eyes. We had front row seat to the ostentatious lifestyle of the rich and famous, racial tensions, superb education, cultural diversity, economic prosperity, booming middle class, democracy at work, poverty in the midst of plenty, and many other first impressions. We arrived at the time that apartheid was still in the news. We were pleasantly surprised by the extensive anti- apartheid sentiment on the campus and in the nation as a whole, institutions and corporations diversifying their investments from banks and other entities associated with the apartheid regime of South Africa. On the contrary, we were sorely disappointed to hear some key Christian leaders speaking in support of the US government's position, which at that time was favorable to the oppressive South African regime.

Theresa arrived in August, the tail end of summer. Soon, the fall season started. I had already experienced one cycle of Michigan weather, so it was my turn to help her navigate the weather system. The joke in the State was that Michigan has three seasons - winter, winter and winter. Sometimes, we were thrilled to experience the phenomenon of "Indian summer," a short period of unseasonably warm or mild weather that occurs in later autumn or early winter. We quickly learned the tricks of keeping warm in winter - bundling up in layers upon layers of clothes, versus just one thick outer covering. We purchased "Long Johns" undergarment to help and acquired the taste of dressing up in the iconic American outfit – blue jeans. We enjoyed the fluffy stuff, but also had our fair share of accidents in the inclement weather. We slipped and fell a couple of times, thankfully without any major injuries.

After some of the euphoria of the reunion had worn off, it was time to face the realities of living in America as a couple. Both Theresa and I found that being out of the country did not mean good riddance of our homeland. After all, some of our siblings, and other loved ones remained in Ghana. We had to keep the communication lines open. The thing about being oceans away is that every phone call from home makes one anxious, for it could bear good or bad news. The challenge of keeping long distance relationships is not being able to respond immediately to needs and emergencies.

America is the land of opportunity, we are told. So, where is the opportunity in the midst of all these complexities of life in America? We realized quickly that, if this was to happen, it was up to us. We had to create our own opportunities and/or avail ourselves of what was available. We determined to make it in America and that meant devising a plan for the future. The plan was simple and strategic:

1. **"Us" first** – We took a vow to live together as one and give ourselves to each other. After a year apart, it was critical to recalibrate and put our union back on a sound foundation. We had to reaffirm our commitment to each other as our highest priority, so we could commit to other things going forward as one to pursue common goals, knowing that we would have each other's back, through thick and thin. There will be no hidden agendas. There were immediate needs to take care of, and some that could be delayed. Theresa needed to get health insurance as a matter of urgency, so that was immediately addressed.

2. **Sound financial base** – My Fulbright Fellowship was designed to support just one person. We needed additional source(s) of income to support the two of us. My J-1 visa prohibited me from accepting additional employment. So, Theresa was the person to seek additional income. Because of her training in Ghana, this was a natural undertaking that she was eager and pleased to pursue.

3. **Raising a family** – As previously indicated, having

33

children was a top priority for us, as it is for married couples in Ghana. This made broadening our financial base even more important. We knew having children will complicate our lives as we pursued our educational interests. But, again, Theresa had been prepared for hard work and multitasking through her upbringing.

4. **Professional development** – We came to the US primarily because of my graduate studies. But Theresa is a smart lady with career aspirations that needed to be nurtured and supported. There was no need to abandon her dreams if there was opportunity to advance her education. In fact, one distinct hope we had was that the US would be the place for her dream of a career in medicine to come true.

5. **Preparing to go back home** – When we had completed our education, we had to return home to serve our country. We needed to plan to make the return as smooth as possible.

6. **Assisting those at home** – It is normal for folks back home to expect their family members in America, "God's country", where milk and honey is supposed to flow, to assist those back home as much as possible.

7. **Remaining in legal immigration status** – Nothing could be done if we fell out of immigration status. We determined to play it by the books so we would not have to look over our shoulders at any time.

This is only a sketch of our plan to guide how we were going to live in America. Of course things could change anytime, but it was wise to have a rough guide so that we did not shoot from the hip. Further, the plan was not meant to be followed in the order it is currently written, as any of the items could become top priority at any time, and also new ones could be added. This was an ambitious strategic plan, but we were determined to make it happen, with God's help of course.

Chapter 6

Working Our Plan

here is a popular Akan saying that translates to: "We did not come to look at the sea; we came to work." Theresa and I did not come to America as tourists; we came primarily for education. We knew right from the onset that we had no more than five years in which to accomplish this primary aim. However long that we intended to stay, if we had to make it in America, we had to develop and work our plan. We had to work together as a team towards achieving well-defined goals and objectives.

To be successful at executing our plan, it was imperative that we understood the nature of the lay of the land or playing field, the rules and regulations for playing, support systems and, opportunities available; and also learn from others how to navigate the complex social landscape of America for success. People come to America with very high and sometimes unrealistic hopes and expectations. Though I had traveled extensively before coming to America, it still offered its surprises to me, and also to Theresa. The secondhand information from people who've been here and through the wide variety of media outlets may be useful, but nothing compares to a firsthand experience. Some of the surprises were positive and helpful to us on our journey through life in the US; others were unpleasant. Either way, we had to adjust quickly and adapt to make the best of every situation. I will share specific experiences (you might say culture shock) and discuss how we handled or took advantage of them, to stretch our budget

First, we had to take care of the basics, getting our house in order. We needed to get our health and general wellbeing taken care of as a matter of high priority. We had to ensure that we had funds to take care of food, rent and the bare necessities of life. We learned quickly that it was very expensive to get sick in America. Consequently, we had to be covered by health insurance. My fellowship provided for health insurance for only me and so we had to purchase one for Theresa. My stipend was designed to support one person, so a top priority for us was how to improve our financial resources. As a Fulbright Scholar on a J-1 visa, I was forbidden to work for extra income. However, Theresa, a J-2, could work, so she had to go out and work, something she was more than eager to do. The training she received at home from her mother and grandmother, as well as the boarding school experience made Theresa independent, self-reliant, a good home manager, entrepreneur, go-getter, determined, disciplined and well- mannered. She arrived with a strong foundation in education.

A key component of our plan was starting a family. We did not want to postpone this high priority goal any further. Then, of course, was the matter of Theresa's professional development. She was not only a very smart person, but she had an ambition to become a professional lady. More specifically, she had a dream of pursuing a career in medicine, with the ultimate goal of helping to alleviate the suffering of people and challenges in the healthcare system back home, as it pertains to poor and disadvantaged women. This dream had not come true in Ghana. Was America, the land of opportunity, the place for it to be realized? Another important component of the plan was how to assist family members whom we left behind. Unfortunately, as at writing, none of our parents were living. But we had siblings and other relatives who needed or expected help from us.

The following are some of the early information we obtained to help us navigate the American society wisely and to our advantage:

Garage sales: Waking up on a Saturday morning, walking through the neighborhood or driving around town, and seeing garage fronts, roadsides, and neighborhood yards filled with tables laden with used household items was new to us. In Ghana, people sell items, especially, big ticket ones like cars, TVs, etc. by word of mouth, by the roadside, or at storefronts. Selling household items like kitchen utensils, and personal effects (e.g., clothing and accessories) in the open, was not a cultural practice we were used to. In hard times, some people in Ghana sell personal items, but do so privately. As students, after we got used to it, we stretched our budget by buying many things at garage sales. In fact, the entire residential complex for students was one giant perpetual garage sale. Students who had completed their studies and were about to depart from the campus, advertised their household stuffs for sale.

Store sales: Whether it was true or not, seeing items marked down from say $100.00 to $25.00, was incredulous. We learned quickly that buying things out of season (buy summer things in winter and *vice versa*) was a wise thing to do. I write elsewhere in this book to celebrate Theresa's shopping skills. We found the "$ xx.99" labels, e.g., "$19.99" or "$99.99," amusing.

Used clothes for sale: Used clothes for sale was really nothing new to us. In Ghana, there are sections in markets, especially, in cities and large towns that are devoted to selling used clothes from America. We did not expect that selling used clothes would be common place in the US. People who buy used clothes back home are not highly regarded. Of course, we wore hand-me- downs from our family members, but never went out to buy used clothes. That said, one of the first stores we visited in the US, was the Goodwill Store (Salvation Army second hand store) to purchase used winter clothes and various household items.

Hunger and free food: Free food in the US was not a shock to us. After all, we were used to the non-fat milk, yellow corn meal, wheat flour, soybean oil, and other food items that were frequently distributed via USAID and missionaries to needy people. What was a shock to us was learning that yes, even in the king's house, people were hungry. The sight of people rummaging through trash cans, and people camped at feeding stations like soup kitchens for food, was unexpected. "If you have so much food to send tons of it all over the world, how can there be hunger in your own backyard?" we thought. That said, we took advantage of free food, whenever it was made available to us, such as when we were offered assistance through the WIC (Women Infants and Children) program when our children were born and our budget was tight.

Poverty: Homeless people sleeping on street curbs and under overpasses, and begging at street corners in the US? The disparity in society was overwhelming - extremely rich and extremely poor. We found that some high schools in suburban areas could rival our universities in Ghana in terms of instructional technology. On the other hand, some high schools in urban or inner city areas were surprisingly poorly equipped for a nation that is a world leader in education. We were shocked by programs on TV that showed people in the Southern US living in conditions that were at the standard of developing countries. We soon learned that poverty was no respecter of persons and could strike at short notice. A person could lose a job and be immediately forced out of his or her house for defaulting on the mortgage payment.

Store coupons: The availability and use of coupons to reduce the grocery bill as well as the cost of shopping at the malls was a new concept to us. In Ghana, we were used to haggling for almost anything. A seller was almost always requested and expected to reduce the selling price or increase the quantity of the item if possible. Theresa learned to be a master coupon clipper, thereby reducing our grocery bills significantly.

All you can eat buffet: There are various formats of eateries in Ghana. However, at the time we left home, the concept of "all you can eat" restaurants was alien. Entering a restaurant in the US and being greeted by row upon row of dishes from which one may gorge oneself for one price, was new to us, but a pleasant surprise. We utilized this outlet as often as we needed to, especially, on weekends after church.

Sue-happy culture: Sue, sue, sue! It was very impressive to see that the judicial system in the US worked reasonably well. However, we were surprised to see how litigious the society is. Law suits were everywhere and for anything. One spills hot coffee on oneself, and then turns around to sue the restaurant for brewing their coffee too hot. Go figure.

TV with 200 or more channels: At the time we left Ghana, that was the early 80s, TV was government-owned. We had just one channel that was operated by the Ghana Broadcasting Corporation (GBC). Then we arrived in the US to find that one could receive over 200 TV channels at home. TV was in color as well. This became a major entertainment outlet for us. We did not have to spend additional funds to attend movies or concerts. We could watch religious programs and educational programs as well, from the comfort of our living room.

Ghana in America: When we left Ghana, the country was experiencing fuel and food shortages. Upon arriving in the US, we were shocked to find that African and other international grocery stores were filled with all kinds of food items from the continent. One could find Ghanaian staples like plantain, *gari*, vegetables, smoked fish, yams...just name it, in international grocery stores. In essence, one could eat like he or she was still back home. Initially, we travelled to larger metropolitan areas to purchase these items, because those were the places we could find international stores.

Part-time quality education: In Ghana, one could pursue some educational programs through correspondence courses offered by overseas educational agencies. There were evening classes for workers. In America, we found that there were numerous avenues available for getting quality and affordable education. More importantly, one could do it at his or her own pace, a course here and there, as it fits into one's work schedule. This was of particular interest to us, considering Theresa's educational plans.

Fast food restaurants: Ghana has a variety of eateries, including the very popular and affordable roadside "chop bars," as well as modern restaurants and hotels. In the evenings, a night market of sellers of all kinds of snacks and quickly prepared foods spring up by the street side, especially, under a street light post, to do business. However, the concept of quick made-to-order foods, with drive-throughs, like McDonalds and Burger King, was new to us. As students, we did not have resources to dine out at fancy restaurants. We supplemented home cooking with burgers and fries as necessary, watching out for coupons for "specials." This provided a quick access to a good meal, when we were pressed for time and low on cash.

Credit card society: The concept of buying things on credit was not new. In Ghana, there is a credit system that is referred to, jokingly, as *san dan ho* (translated "mark on the wall"). I guess in America, the equivalent expression is "keep it on my tab." However, we were surprised to know how commercial banks actually encouraged people to acquire credit via credit cards (plastic), some of them with exorbitant fees. This was an easy way to finance a purchase, but also an easy way to get into debt. I found this out the very hard way later on, when I used credit cards to finance various projects, including book publishing that turned out to be financially unfruitful.

Throwaway society: We learned sooner than later that it was cheaper to buy a new replacement, in some cases, than to repair broken items. We could buy a new pair of shoes cheaper than having one re-soled. Many electronic items were cheaper to dump in the thrash and replace than to repair them. When our car had a slight bumper accident, we chose to live with it rather than repair it, because the whole bumper had to be replaced, not just fixing the dent. In Ghana, almost any part of the car can be mended when in need of repair.

Eat, eat, eat: Everywhere one turned, someone was drinking, licking or chewing something. Even in church, people ate doughnuts and drank coffee! That was really strange to us. Grocery stores had food stations where free samples of selected products that were being promoted were served. We found potlucks and parties were common social events.

Public display of affection: Ghanaians and Africans in general are more reserved in terms of displaying affection in public. On the other hand, hugging is very common and sincere. I call hugging in America, the "half-hug" or "partial hug." I am tall, 6ft 2in to be exact. So, when my pastor's wife always hooked my neck and pulled me down for a hug, I thought it was the height factor. After a while, I noticed that it was a deliberate way to avoid my chest touching her bosom. It became clearer when one day in church a pastor instructed us to "to hug someone's neck" as our welcome greeting of each other. Handshake is perhaps the most common form of greetings in Ghana. Male friends usually cap a handshake with a loud snap of the fingers. Kissing, especially in public, is not part of the culture. We were surprised to see kissing almost everywhere and anywhere, including church.

Social security number: We found the magic social security number (SSN) was needed for nearly all major social transactions. It is required for employment and most financial transactions. Don't leave home without it memorized. We also learned that it could be abused, if it got into the hands of identity thieves.

Sensational reporting of the news: More often than not, we found that many TV news stations tended to highlight the negative aspects of the African experience. Even when the news was good, the backdrop was always negative. The stereotypical themes were images of wildlife, extreme poverty, wars and the like. This bias is not limited to the news media. I recall an incidence at church. My pastor had announced that the following Sunday was going to be Mission Sunday. A team he led on a trip to South Africa through

Europe was scheduled to present their trip to the church. I was excited and thought that it was a good opportunity to invite some African friends to church. Wrong. The presentation started well, with shots of nice places and well-dressed people from Europe, the congregation oohing and aahing in response to the photos. When it got to Africa, it was like comedy hour. The first slide was a wall gecko on the wall, followed by a toilet that would not flush properly, etc. The congregation burst out laughing. One of the friends I had invited leaned over and asked: "Is he trying to make fun of these people?" I was very embarrassed. On another occasion in a different church, the pastor who had just come from a missions trip made comments like: "The people stink;" "The children have lost their teeth because they don't brush them;" "I was preaching as monkeys were running all around," We have very high regard for missionaries, for many sacrifice their comfortable living in America to go to various challenging parts of Africa. So for us to hear them talk in the manner they did was disappointing.

Multiple choice questions: We encountered several differences in the educational system that were quite surprising to us. One of the new experiences to us at school was how exams were conducted. In those days in Ghana, exams entailed mostly essay type questions at all levels. It was not enough to provide an answer. The way it was constructed, including grammar, was judged as part of the answer. Commonly, one had forty-five minutes in which to interpret and answer a question. So we were shocked to find that most exams were constructed as true or false, multiple choice, or fill in the blanks. Suffice it to say that many of us from Africa struggled initially with these exams, until we got the hang of it.

Issues in education - We were not used to college classifications and rankings – first tier, second tier, etc.; top 50, top 100 universities or academic programs; Big Ten, Ivy League; accredited or unaccredited; regional vs comprehensive; research I; etc. It was prestigious to study at or have your child study at an Ivy League university, just like one of our children, Bozuma, did. We were, and continue to be, dismayed at the disparity in the access to quality education in America. Public schools in urban areas, which are usually dominated by Blacks and other minorities, are poorer in quality of resources

The foregoing are some of our early experiences that may be described as cultural shock. Of course we did not have to learn or experience all the above before launching our plan. Theresa decided, first, to secure a job, any job, to help with the upkeep of the family. Associated with finding a job is a means of transportation to get to and from work. The winters in Michigan are severe. The campus buses helped quite a bit, but if one had to work off campus, and particularly late at night, or work multiples jobs, one needed to own a car or have a friend who'd help by providing the needed transportation. We purchased a jalopy, a Chevy, for about $400.00. We got it from the popular campus car market.

Theresa's first job was in my department, courtesy of my professor. Her daily task was cleaning bean samples in the Bean Research Program. It paid minimum wage, but every dollar was appreciated. She did not have to put her career on hold on my account. So, in October of her first year in the US, she enrolled in two graduate classes, in the hope of getting into a graduate program at the earliest opportunity. In the meantime, she ordered copies of her college transcripts from UCC. Theresa A-ced the two courses. This was powerful evidence that she could handle a rigorous graduate program. She applied and was promptly admitted into an MS program in Plant Breeding and Genetics. Without enough funds, she could only pursue her program on a part time basis.

Part of our plan was to start a family. Now that Theresa was established in a graduate program, it was time to pay more attention to having and raising children. The details of this aspect of our lives are the subject of the next chapter. During the MS program, Theresa's desire to go to medical school was rekindled by a vivid dream. In this dream, she saw herself in a physician's white coat, with a stethoscope around her neck, rounding on patients with her good friend Ivy Dankwa Ekem, a physician in Ghana. She acted on the dream and approached the admissions office of the Michigan

State University Medical School program. That is when she learned that she could not be admitted into a medical program without US citizenship or at least a Green Card (aka, permanent residency). With that news, we decided that she should settle for a PhD program. During her MS program, she conducted research that made her fall in love with fungal studies. She successfully completed the MS program after about two years. She enrolled in a PhD program in Plant Pathology. But after about six months, her major advisor left her position to assume a demanding administrative role. Thank God, Dr. Donald Ramsdel stepped in as the new major advisor. Unfortunately, he did not have funds to award her graduate assistantship. To support her studies, Theresa had to work in the Physical Plant department from 9.00 pm to 1.00 am, cleaning classrooms. One of the challenging courses in the program was a physiology class with a reputation for "no one gets an A in this class." Well, tell that to Theresa. Her earlier scores for homework assignments were 8 out of 10. She needed to score more 10/10 to earn an A. Later, Dr. Ramsdel awarded her work study support. Not having to work late nights any more allowed her to spend more time in the library. Without working late hours, she spent her time in the library. She ended up with an A in the class! The work study was short-lived.

She was offered a Teaching Assistantship for the remainder of her program.

I graduated in 1987 with a PhD in Plant Breeding and Genetics. Alas, the primary reason for which we came to the US had been accomplished!! We thanked God for this major milestone. Now, we faced huge decisions. Theresa was in the middle of her graduate work; we had children whose birth circumstances required them to continue to receive developmental health intervention and preschool education. I had used up about four of my allowable five years under my fellowship. Because I had completed my studies, I needed permission to continue to stay in country, even for the purpose of the allowable practical experience. I had less than one year of practical experience before my visa expired.

44

The only way to extend my stay in the US was to apply for visa extension. For a J-1 visa, this could be done only outside the country. I had to either return to Ghana and reapply for reentry, or seek such accommodation through a US embassy in another country. The closest and least expensive option was Canada. I took the chance and travelled to Toronto to apply for a J-1 extension to complete the work experience after my studies. If unsuccessful, I would have been denied reentry into the US, and would have been compelled to leave from Toronto straight back to Ghana! Thank God, I was approved for legal stay for the remainder of the time on my original visa.

With a new lease on life, I returned triumphantly to continue my work. I was offered a post-doctoral fellowship in the USDA Sugar Beets Genetics Lab on campus, working with Dr. Joe Saunders. Later I worked in the Bean/ Cowpea CRISP program under Dr. Adams as a Visiting Research Associate. Just when we thought things were back to normal, my major advisor retired from the university. The CRISP project was relocated to UC Davis. The new program director sent me a memo one day instructing me to stop work, pack all samples, and ship them promptly to his lab. And just like that I was out of work. I had about eight months left on my visa. As a J-1 visa holder, I could not work outside the campus. We were experiencing firsthand the American reality that anyone can suddenly be plunged into poverty, and even become homeless, with the slightest misfortune. In our case, my wife still had her fellowship. With a wife and three children and her mother living with us, I needed to find a job, and rather quickly, too.

The good news of a job came within about a week. A friend of ours, Dr. Chongo Mundende, who was working at Langston University in Oklahoma, knocked on our door, unexpectedly. A position had come open in his program. He had convinced his boss that he knew just the right person for it. He had arrived on a mission. Theresa was not available to take the offer. She did not hesitate to shove me out of the door to pursue the opportunity. And so, in 1991, I left East Lansing, Michigan, for Langston, Oklahoma, to begin our second family separation in the US.

Theresa had to adjust quickly to pick up the slack. Her mother was around, but she had health challenges that did not allow her to provide the customary support that married women receive from their mothers in Ghana. Theresa was determined to multitask without putting the children at risk. She eliminated most social activities from her schedule. The children were enrolled in various after-school activities, including swimming, golf, tennis, guitar and piano lessons, activities that had age-dependent schedules. Later, she synchronized the piano and guitar lessons so that the children could simultaneously take lessons at one location.

The academic load, all of a sudden, was compounded by the additional load of family matters. Theresa recalls how she had to be the first at the door of the daycare center so she could literally shove one kid, Bozuma, in and make a dash to the campus to be punctual for TA duties, which started at eight o'clock. Sometimes, she had to stay late in the lab to attend to her research. One early morning, she could not return home early enough to get the children ready for school, but could not interrupt her work. She stayed for as long as possible and then made a mad dash for home. To her surprise our oldest son, Parry, just about seven years old, child, had the presence of mind to take it upon himself to wake up his younger sister, wash and dress her, while waiting for Mom to return!

I lived with Chongo at the beginning of my stay in Oklahoma. I visited on holidays. The separation was challenging, but a more serious problem that was looming was my immigration status. It did not take long for my J-1 visa extension to run out. I was served with voluntary departure notice by the US Immigration Service. Being out of status meant being out of work, for my employer could not continue to hire me without proper documentation. I sought the assistance of an immigration lawyer to plead my case. The basis of the appeal was hardship to my US-born children who were receiving medical and educational interventions related to the events at the times of their birth. An application was filed with the US immigration service. After a couple of weeks, the denial came, and this time with a shorter window of time within which to voluntarily depart or be forcibly deported.

Theresa had by that time completed her MS and enrolled in a PhD program. She had to switch to a J-1 visa for the purpose of continuing her graduate education. Unfortunately, I could not just automatically extend my J-1 visa under the provisions of her new J-1 visa. This time, I had to depart voluntarily or be deported. Dr. Phil Carey, a professor and friend I made at Langston suggested I petition the US Embassy in Bahamas, his native country for the J-2 visa. I could stay with his brother during the process. It was quite a challenge to secure the switch in immigration status. But eventually, I was granted a new J-2 visa, based on the time left on Theresa's J-1 visa. Thank God, again.

I returned to the US with a new lease on life and a spring in my step. Theresa recalls later that when I returned to visit after being away for several months, she could not bear to look at me for I was as skinny as a flag pole and looked sickly. The children were progressing well in school, receiving developmental education and physical therapy on the side. We decided it was time to file for permanent residency again to bring some stability into the family life. We did so, and thank God, we were successful after a long process. What a big relief that was! It would be three years before we would be reunited in Oklahoma. We were now more certain about where we would call home and raise our family, at least for the foreseeable future. I indicated earlier that Theresa had always wanted a large family, six children, to be exact. So, on one of my visits to Michigan, we decided to go for child number four. Can you image taking care of three children and a mother with health challenges, being pregnant, and still working towards the completion of a challenging PhD program? We'll, that is the kind of stuff Theresa is made of. Call her "Wonder Woman" and you will not be exaggerating.

Theresa worked hard and completed her PhD in Plant Pathology on 8/22/94. Some of the great friends she made during the period of her doctoral studies included Ray Pacovsky and Thanda Wai. With a full time job and a more dependable income, I rented an apartment in Guthrie, Oklahoma, about 15 minutes' drive from my workplace, Langston University. Another good friend I made earlier on at Langston University was Evelyn Weekes. We both loved publishing; we also collaborated on grants. Later, I moved into a house in Edmond, in preparation for the arrival of the rest of the family.

When they arrived, Theresa took a year off before accepting a position as Assistant Professor in the Department of Biology at my institution. On September 8th, 1994, our fourth child, Tina, was born. Some of the subjects discussed in this chapter will be revisited and addressed in greater detail in ensuing chapters, so as to make them more relevant to Theresa's story and more powerful.

Chapter 7

Having Children

Most married couples look forward to having children at some point in life. The time when children come into the equation and the number of them depend on several factors including health, income, career and religious beliefs, to name a few. In societies and communities in which the knowledge and practice of birth control are nonexistent or limited, marriages tend to result in quite a few children. In Ghana, family sizes of between four and six (including parents) are common, especially among the educated. Larger numbers prevail in the rural areas.

In the US and other Western societies, some educated women struggle with advancing their professional careers and raising a family at the same time. Some put off having children until they are well established in their careers. When they have children, they limit the number to one or two. Some choose not to have children at all, so they may devote full attention to their careers. When African women marry, having children is always a top priority. Theresa's achievements are more impressive when you consider the circumstances under which she accomplished them. Yes, she wanted to advance her academic and professional careers. Even more important to her was raising a family. For her, it was not an either/or proposition. She wanted to pursue both, simultaneously. When we reunited after one year, and decided to make up for lost time, it was not just fun and games. We wanted to start a family as soon as possible. I was in my early 30s; she was past mid-20s. So, in the first year of our reunion, we set our plan in motion. We found out soon enough that bringing children into the world, in the US, was not a matter to be taken lightly. In addition to regular health insurance, we needed to have pregnancy insurance. The truth of the matter is that before we could purchase the proper insurance something was already cooking in the oven. The joyful news came one morning when Theresa experienced the customary morning sickness while brushing her teeth. It was one early September morning, just as we were getting ready for school. Of course, we were ecstatic that our dream of having children was coming true! At the same time, we were concerned about what was to come in about nine months, not the precious gift of life alone, but the expenses associated with it. In fact, before touchdown, there were months of prenatal care.

We did not immediately announce the pregnancy to the world. This is not a customary practice in Ghana. We waited for observers to find out in due course, as the signs manifested. Dr. Fred Settler, her co-major advisor, awarded her a quarter-time research assistantship, not because of the pregnancy, though. He, like all others, found out later. The award enabled her to qualify for in- state tuition. Consequently, she decided to convert to a full-time graduate program. Her tasks in the lab included preparing culture media and cleaning the tons of glassware used in the pathology lab by the researchers. She could handle this while sitting at the sink.

Without pregnancy insurance, we were left with taking advantage of the free services provided for low income people by Logan County. Without a car of our own at that time, Theresa depended on the goodwill of friends and public transportation for all the prenatal hospital visits, sometimes standing outside for long times in the Michigan winter. For a person who had not travelled out of the country prior to coming to the US, standing at the bus stop in the severe winter, with tons of snow all over the place and sometimes walking in blizzards while pregnant, was a daunting experience. Later on, a friend of ours, Joe Ofori Dankwa, offered to drive her to subsequent prenatal appointments.

D-day came four weeks too soon. On May 9th, 1985, Theresa had scheduled a regular doctor's appointment. Unfortunately, her ride cancelled at the last minute because of a conflict of schedule.

Theresa insisted on keeping the appointment and went by public transportation. Wise decision! At that visit, it was determined that she had highly elevated blood pressure, preeclampsia as doctors call it. She was rushed to the hospital for emergency delivery by Cesarean delivery, four weeks ahead of her due date, at the Sparrow Hospital, East Lansing, Michigan. Behold, our first son was born, and we called him Parry, a 5 lb four-week "premie". "For our first child, we'll take it, any way he came," we said to ourselves. I got the good news, albeit a huge surprise, while in the lab working on my doctoral research project. Parry spent one week in the Neonatal Intensive Care Unit (NICU) before leaving for home with us. Our hospital bill was huge, since we had no pregnancy insurance. However, because it was determined that the premature birth was caused by preeclampsia, a health condition, our health insurance covered most of the charges, leaving us with the co-pay. Thank God.

Naming of children in Ghana is a family affair in most parts of Ghana. Of course, the child will assume the last name of the father, or be named completely after him. However, the couple receives input from the extended family for the middle name(s). The couple usually decides to name the child after their parents, first, and also grandparents or other people in the family whom they hold in high regard. In our case, we took a middle of the road approach, naming him after me and my dad, Shiloh Parry Osafo, hence his name George Parry Acquaah. In fact, the proper spelling of the middle name, in our native tongue, is "Opare," not Parry (a corruption by the British).

The naming of a child occurs one week after birth, and is usually a very special occasion for the family. A family elder performs the traditional ceremony. One very interesting aspect of the ceremony is when the child is prayed for and admonished to grow up to be a wise person who can distinguish between right and wrong, and not give in to deceit. For symbolism, the officiant (usually an elder family member) dips a finger first into a glass of water and touches the lips of the child, followed by touching the lips after dipping into a glass of hard liquor. During the "forced tasting," the elder may say something like: "This is water, and this is alcohol. Know the difference between the two and be wise in your ways." Another custom is male circumcision. Most tribes follow this time-honored tradition of removing the foreskin from the male genital. Some prefer it to be done by "traditional surgeons" (called *Wanzam*) from the Muslim community for whom this is a requirement, and are deemed to be more skillful at this operation than Western-trained doctors. We did not have any options in this matter and decided to have it done in the hospital before the baby went home. I was required to witness the procedure live, not to mention the gut-wrenching scream of my baby in agony, as no anesthetic was used.

We could not wait to have mother and child home to start a new phase in our lives. Suddenly, we were responsible for a fragile human being. We had to factor him into our schedules, giving him special concessions and privileges. Theresa would have to learn to mother an infant all by herself. Back home in Ghana, a new mother is usually pampered by relatives. The woman's mother may choose to come and live with her daughter for several weeks and even months, showing her the ropes of childcare, and most importantly, relieving the new mother of the nursing roles in the first couple of weeks. The new mother would be waited upon, as others cook for her and her family. In a strange land, Theresa missed out on these privileges. Instead, she had to combine nursing a new child with studies and work.

The first child, they say, is a novel experience for the couple. The child tends to be pampered and even sometimes spoiled rotten. We took photos of Parry's every move. We bought him every toy imaginable and clothes galore. Of course, with a new mouth to feed, our budget was stretched thinner yet. We took advantage of all the social services available in Logan County, including the WIC (Women Infants and Children) program, which provided supplemental food for women and infants. We had to purchase a car so that we did not have to be dependent on friends to transport us to the regular hospital visits that followed.

During the latter part of her MS program, Theresa became pregnant with our second child, Kwasi. This was upon the recommendation of our OB/GYN physician. We were planning to return home upon completion of our programs. Just in case there might be some complications with subsequent pregnancies, our doctor recommended that we try to have another baby before leaving the US. His recommendation was spot on. Kwasi's birth was even more eventful than Parry's. We were very thankful we heeded the doctor's advice. He was born on November 30th, 1986, by C-section as well, ten weeks premature and weighing only 4.8 lbs. This time, it was also determined that a tumor in Theresa's parathyroid gland was at least a contributing factor to the complications at the birth of Kwasi. He was named after my dad –

Kwasi Osafo Acquaah. In fact, I am the only one in the family who goes by the Acquaah name; all others have our dad's name – Osafo. I was named after Rev. Acquaah, my dad's uncle. The Osafo name was never used at any time, even when I started school. So, I wanted to revive that important link and hence included the name in our family tree by at least naming one of the children Osafo.

Taking care of full-term infants is a challenge; caring for a ten-week premie is even more a daunting task. Kwasi spent about three weeks in the NICU and was eventually released into our care. He came home on an apnea monitor, for he had not recovered completely from the developmental challenges associated with his birth circumstances. It was cheaper to care for him at home at this stage, than to remain in intensive care. For about six months, we had to get use to the monitor beeping every so often to alert us of Kwasi's irregular breathing and heartbeat. Poor Theresa had to cope with the stress of motherhood and the challenges of a rigorous graduate school program. She had to care for Parry, who was under two years, and now Kwasi with all the medical challenges, and also pursue her studies. She was constantly confronted with the question by inquiring minds: "Theresa, how do you do it?" Of course, even though I was waist deep in my doctoral program, I provided the needed support at home. We tried to minimize the use of daycare for the children by taking turns to babysit them at home. Unfortunately, there was a time that I had to travel to Chicago for a critical professional meeting. Parry had to be taken to a babysitter for the first time, so Theresa could attend classes. This experience was traumatic for him and we the parents. He cried all the time until his mother came to the rescue after school. In his mother's bosom at last, Parry planted his head firmly into her arms, and sobbed uncontrollably. Upon hearing this gut-wrenching occurrence, I took the next flight back home right away! Nothing was that important to sacrifice for my son.

Theresa's tumor was eventually removed, but not without anxious moments, as the doctors had to send it out for additional expert opinion as to its nature. After several weeks of waiting, we were informed that it was benign. We were very thankful to God for being in a country with a sophisticated healthcare system that saved the lives of both mother and child! Theresa was not particularly dismayed by her health challenges. She sports a thin long scar in the lower neck region from the surgery that was done to remove the tumor, and vows to keep it as a memorial to the goodness of God, she says.

Our hospital bill was a mile long. We had medical insurance as well as pregnancy insurance that took care of a significant portion of the charges. We were advised to apply for Medicaid to assist with the balance of Kwasi's unpaid bills. One of the health providers failed to bill Medicaid directly, choosing instead to send the bill to us. Of course, we could not pay. Consequently, our bill was sent to a collections agency to squeeze us for as much as they could. With this blemish on our records, we found it very hard to obtain a credit card later on. Welcome to America! We had to work hard in the following years to repair our credit rating to its current excellent level (840 as at writing).

Parry continued to grow and develop without any visible physical challenges. Kwasi needed several years of physical therapy to correct some minor malformation in his lower limbs. Because of their premature births, we were notified that it would be at school-going age before we would know if the stress at birth may have caused developmental challenges that could adversely impact their learning. They were automatically enrolled in developmental learning programs with regular monitoring for delayed learning and other deficiencies.

Through it all, on no occasion did I sense that Theresa had

second thoughts about her challenging and full life. On the contrary, she appeared like a woman on a mission. She had a plan and was working it hard. She was willing to delay gratification and sacrifice to get what she wanted. The problem was that a woman could pay attention to the children to the detriment of her personal needs, not to mention those of her husband's. Theresa frequently invoked her favorite "sacrificing for the kids" mantra. I called it "pleading the marital 5th." She would often say: "I cannot afford to leave the kids with anyone to go and have fun. How can I look myself in the face or explain to anyone, should something bad happen to them while I was out having fun?" This posture was admirable, but it meant that we had less quality time together as husband and wife. We seldom went out together for entertainment of any kind. Not that we had plenty of free time anyway, considering that we were both graduate students in demanding programs.

It has already been stated that Theresa loves children and wanted to have a house full of them. So, notwithstanding the complications at childbirth associated with the first two children, she was determined to proceed according to plan. This time, it was clear that we had to avail ourselves of the superior healthcare system in the US before going home. Were there any more surprises to come? Would future pregnancies continue to be progressively complicated? We went ahead and loaded the oven one more time. Six months into her doctoral program, she became pregnant with our third child. With each pregnancy, came a mixture of concern and admiration for Theresa from colleagues and others. Sometimes we felt like our American friends just could not figure us out. "What is wrong with these people?", it felt like some were saying. "How can you pursue a rigorous doctoral program while pregnant, and raise two young children at the same time?" her colleagues often wondered.

With an additional mouth to feed, Theresa took on additional work with the Physical Plant division, working from 9 pm - 1.00 am, as previously indicated. I was forbidden to work, and so any additional income had to come via her efforts. Taking classes, working late hours, and running a family was very challenging, to say the least. One night, she was broad-sided by another driver on her way back home from work. Theresa was not one to slack on her academic work. Dr. Ramsdel came through again with a work study offer. Consequently, she stopped the night work to concentrate on her studies and family life. On November 9th, 1989, our first daughter, Bozuma, was born. She was full term, weighing in at 9lb 3oz, and delivered vaginally, after two previous C- sections! Praise the Lord. She was named after my mother-in-law, with the encouragement and blessing of my father. Born on Thursday, we added her day name, Yaa (a boy would be Yaw) – and hence her name, Yaa Bozuma Acquaah. Theresa also had a brief stint at the Kellogg Center, a hotel built to support the hotelier program at MSU. She started at the checkout counter but was too slow in that role and was hence sent to work in the kitchen doing dishes and other jobs.

I had to leave Michigan suddenly for Oklahoma, as previously stated. I had a wife and three kids and was unemployed. This was beginning to sound like the lyrics of a country song. What a predicament to be in. The separation was for about three years. Theresa was on a quest to fulfil her goal in the area of having children. So, during the year prior to reuniting in Oklahoma, we decided to initiate yet another pregnancy. I am certain by this time our American colleagues and friends thought we had "lost our marbles." To her credit, Theresa is not one to be overly bothered by what others think or say about her. She has her life to live, and she was determined to live it according to her plan. She completed her PhD and joined me in Oklahoma, eventually. We resided at our first single family home located at an address in Chowing Heights, in Edmond. Then, on September 8th, 1994, we were blessed with another bouncing baby girl, also vaginally delivered and weighing in at 8lb 11oz. She was the only "Okie" among three "Lakers." She was born at the Oklahoma University Hospital. It looks like the girls made up for the weight the boys did not have at birth.

Theresa's mother left for Ghana in September of 1992, before she left Michigan to join me in Oklahoma. With four beautiful children, two boys and two girls, it looked like it was time to call it a day with having children. We thanked God and closed that chapter in our lives, focusing now on raising them the best way possible.

Chapter 8

Preparing Children for Life:

Lion Mom

Having children is one thing; raising them is quite another. Generally, parents want their children to be highly successful, even beyond what they have achieved themselves. So, what is success? For us, we want all our children to have a strong Christian foundation, first and foremost. We believe that life has purpose. With good Christian upbringing, we expect the children to be persons of integrity and moral uprightness, who are globally aware and civically responsible. Faith is most convincing when it is modelled. As educators who know the value of education, we want our children to be as highly educated as possible. Just like our faith, we model excellence in education to our children. We do not impose our professional preferences on them either; we provide guidance and assistance for them to pursue excellence and become all they can be. Slothfulness is not tolerated.

Theresa's approach to raising children can be characterized by the following attributes – "Lion Mom," sacrificial, relentless, loving, protective, caring and leading by example, among many others. These qualities will be substantiated in due course in this book. Theresa really loves her children and does not hesitate to put them first in many things. To do this means that she sacrifices at every turn, so their needs are met. I introduce the expression "Lion Mom" to contrast Amy Chou's description of the "Asian Tiger Mom," and proudly

57

apply it, for the first time ever, to Theresa, my wife.

Raising children in America is very expensive. Theresa and I came together on our own volition to be husband and wife; the children were brought into the world by us. Therefore, we are responsible for them, until they are independent. For parents who were students managing on meager stipends, the only way to do this was to be frugal and sacrificial in our lifestyle. This is where Theresa shines most brightly. I did not have to suggest it to her, she insisted on it. We embarked on various cost-cutting strategies to stretch our budget. As previously stated, we took advantage of all that was available to us through various social assistance programs in the country. On traditional holidays like Christmas and Thanksgiving, Theresa was not too proud to queue up for a free turkey and other food packets when the charity truck pulled into Spartan Village, our residential quarters at Michigan State. Residents were predominantly internationals, and hence were easy targets for charitable acts on festive occasions.

When other ladies had weekly appointments with their hair dresser, Theresa did her own hair dressing 98% of the time, and the girls' as well. The girls always looked gorgeous in the crowd. Theresa was not given to makeups and manicures. Thank God she is naturally very beautiful and does not need to compensate with artificial supplements. However, a little something every now and then would not have hurt, though. She was not given to adornment with jewelry, just a few basic ones. She turned deaf ears to the occasional pleas from her mother and me to do something for herself every now and then, and to indulge in some of these pleasures. This sacrificial lifestyle did not prevail only while she was a student. In fact, when she started work as an Assistant Professor at Langston University, one colleague of mine informed me about a gossip going around at one time that "Dr. Acquaah always wears the same pair of red shoes." Theresa laughed and brushed it off when I told her about it. Her car had no hub caps. So what?, she'd brush it off. The kids had abundant clothes for all seasons and all occasions. Their education was on track. They had all the toys they desired. The family was very well fed. For Theresa, it was a lifestyle of delayed gratification. With

58

time, as the family finances improved, she approached life differently, albeit still remaining modest but classy.

Theresa is very family-oriented. Almost everything she organizes is for the entire family. She seldom organizes anything for herself or for just the two of us – husband and wife. In a previous chapter I noted her mantra: "I cannot afford to leave the kids behind to go out to have fun. What will I say if something bad happens to them while I was out having fun?" Date nights and getaways were alien concepts to us when the children were home with us. We went out to movies, theater, restaurants, and on vacations together, as a family. Of course, as a man, I was not entirely happy about this lifestyle, but did understand and supported her. Maybe, as the children become adults and more independent, we might then have the house and our calendars to ourselves. But by then somethings might be less fun to do! To ground them in our faith, we did all the routine things – attend church, Bible studies, vacation Bible school, etc.

Academics was also of very high priority for us, not because we are both highly educated, but education opens doors to opportunity. To be competitive in society, we wanted the children to have the best education possible. We were particular about giving them a solid foundation in the basics – reading, English, and mathematics. Parry and Bozuma continue to be avid readers as adults. We encouraged and supported the children to make use of summer special sessions to improve in all these basics. They participated in various specialized after-school supplemental educational programs for children (e.g., Kumon). They had home computers and computer-based learning modules. Theresa was exceptional at supervising homework and making sure the children studied on a regular basis.

It was important for us to have the children well-rounded in their education, and personal growth and development like other children. They enjoyed summer activities – going to amusement parks, sports camps, as well as taking lessons in swimming, *Tae kwon do* and basketball. As parents, this meant traveling with them all over the State of Oklahoma to competitions. Parry and Bozuma were very good at swimming. They won many competitive honors in that sport. All the children took piano lessons. At some point, we had the teacher come to the house to give them lessons to cut down on chauffeuring them all over the place. The boys participated in the Air Force JROTC program and played in the marching band in high school. Kwasi loved everything to do with space. He attended a NASA space camp, as well as a national leadership conference in Washington DC.

Our children grew up in mostly White neighborhoods. We spent about fourteen years in Edmond, Oklahoma, after about ten years in East Lansing, Michigan, where three of them were born. It was important for us to let them know and appreciate their Ghanaian heritage, in addition to the heritage of the land of their birth, America. In elementary school, they always marched in parades in Ghanaian traditional attires, during the International Day celebrations. We did not insist on them learning any particular Ghanaian language. Considering the fact that they had challenges at birth and had to enroll in years of developmental education to correct delayed speech for example, our choice, and wisely so, was to let them be grounded in English so they would be competitive in the US.

We raised our children to have a healthy respect for people of all races and to be globally engaged. The two girls, Bozuma and Tina, participated in People to People programs, touring many countries in Europe. We took all of them to Ghana a couple of times, to visit with family members and also to experience, life in their ancestral home, firsthand. Their first trip home occurred in July 1998. We made sure we carried along suitcases of their favorite nonperishable food items, just in case they did not like the local foods. We travelled via Europe, laying over in Frankfurt for seven hours. Their grandparents were especially excited to see their grandchildren for the first time. Sometimes, they had difficulty understanding their American accent. Their cousins were equally thrilled to see them. We arranged for them to tour a variety of cultural and educational sites, including museums of art, famous slave castles, Aburi Botanical Gardens, Tema Harbor, and the popular Kakum Canopy Walk, one of only a few in the world. The canopy walk consists of a network of wood and rope bridges suspended in the canopies of giant forest trees.

Tina was fascinated by live animals – goats, sheep, chickens - that freely roamed the compound. I recall her chasing chickens all over the compound of my brother's residence.

Much as we would like to have the children visit home more often, each family trip of this nature cost us no less than $20,000.00! When travelling with children, one does not want to cut corners by flying on the cheap. The price of tickets varies with the travel season and the airline. We travelled only when the children were out of school and we could synchronize our professional leave times. This meant that the summer time, the peak time for travel, was usually the best for family travel. The individual ticket price for this time is about $2300-2500 for good and reliable airlines, and for schedules with short layovers. For a family of six, the airfare alone amounts to about $15,000. When we travel, we have to take gifts to family and friends, and have funds for entertainment and recreational tours, as well as eventualities. When the children are older and independent, they may visit as often as they desire. Raising our children, it was important that they embraced Ghanaian values that we felt were lacking in the American culture, some of which have been discussed in a previous chapter. A cultural shock to us was the general lack of respect for adults. It was shocking to us to see how some American children talked back to and argued with their parents. Children often call adults by their first name. It is important that our children respect their elders and in fact all others. "Yes mom/dad," "please," and "thank you," were and continue to be part of the Acquaah family lexicon.

Theresa is known by the family as the Talker. She is not talkative, just one who is very concerned about the wellbeing of others and hence cannot remain silent when talking will help. In the lexicon of married couples, the favorite description for persistent and often critical comments from the wife to the husband is "nagging." Theresa is not a nagger in the traditional sense, but an enthusiastic positive talker. She will always say what she thinks needs to be said, if it will help another person. No one in the family is exempt from the talk. Her argument for the persistent, determined and intrusive engagement of her loved ones in their business is that, as she often

61

declares, "If I don't say it, who will?" "If I stay silent and things go wrong, we will all be the worse for it."

"You are my children; I can't stand by and watch you head in the wrong direction." "Until things change, I will continue to talk and talk and talk..." Of course no one likes to be at the receiving end of repetitive reminders about past events, especially, mistakes, and receive cautionary notes, almost incessantly.

However, when all is said and done, she gets the message through, most of the time, for the good of all.

Theresa is the chief family cheerleader for excellence and success, constantly urging the children on with motivating comments like "You can do it," "I know you are very smart." She never lets a teachable moment go waste. When such moments appear while watching TV, everyone knows the Talker will pounce: "Did you see that? She was homeless and now is studying at Harvard." "You see, with determination and focus, you can achieve anything." "Did you hear about so-and-so? He just came from Ghana and hit the books very hard. Now, he is at Yale." "You must sacrifice for your own education and future." "Stop all the friends and going out to concerts business and focus on your studies." The Ben Carson story was a favorite one that got retold, frequently.

An area in which the incessant talking has paid off is dietary habits of the family. Theresa battles with high cholesterol and is hence very particular about fat and oil intake. To keep blood pressure in check, salt is not a good friend of the family's. When Theresa prepares a chicken dish, the skin goes off first, followed by meticulous examination and removal of the last speck of visible fat. One can imagine what happens when after such a labor of love, the food is not eaten but left to potentially go to waste. This seldom happens, though, because of the "waste not want not" mantra that is part of the talk-talk routine repeated around the house. If you put it on your plate, it must go down the hutch. Otherwise, it must be kept in the fridge or freezer for a later time. The problem with this otherwise commendable household management style is that the fridge and freezer sooner or later become cluttered. Children can be picky about food. They like freshly prepared dishes.

Who doesn't? But when both Mom and Dad work full time and combine it with studies, there is no other choice but to go the refrigerate- and-reheat route.

Theresa is a superb cook! I can cook, and do a lot of it at home. During the periods when Theresa was in medical school and residency, I did most of the cooking. Unlike her, I sometimes either hurried the cooking or delayed it. We taught our children to give thanks for all things. They'll always thank mom or dad, depending on who cooked, for the food before eating. One day, when they were much younger, one of them said this to me: "Thank you dad for the food, even though sometimes it is burnt." Who can dispute the honesty of children? Sometimes I served them "burnt offerings," because I am an extreme multi-tasker. It was not uncommon to have food on the stove, be watching a TV program, a book in hand, studying or writing one. Smoke or the scent of something burning signed that the food was cooked, or in some cases, over cooked. That said, the family loves some of my killer dishes and often requests them. I often cook from recipes, the Western style. Theresa is a Ghanaian home-trained cook. Visitors to the house always compliment her culinary skills. Her dinner rolls that she makes from scratch are never enough, since guests always request for parcels to take home. And so is her *nkate nkwan* (peanut butter soup), served with rice balls.

To her credit, the talk-talk routine is very profitable. We are now all diet-conscious. Tina, like mother like daughter, reads all food labels with religious fervor and provides running commentary to reinforce what mom says. Between the two of them, we are talked into toeing the dietary line so we all eat healthily. We prefer foods with less fat and oil, and eat little red meat. Processed foods are almost entirely verboten. You can't enjoy junk food and pastries in peace without the diet-monitoring squad getting in your face in a hurry, making you lose your appetite instantly.

Theresa is unselfish and freely shares her advice with other parents and her family members. She is thrilled when her advice is heeded and children or parents benefit from it. I must admit that I am

63

the "softie" in the family. I tend to cut the children more slack than she does. Like many other children the Acquaah kids did not progress smoothly via a straight line route in the area of education and career development. They made some changes in career paths along the way. It is possible more of the same is yet to come. In fact, sometimes, Theresa second-guesses herself, thinking that things may have been different if only she had been home more of the time, rather than pursuing her career goal of going to medical school. I strongly disagree, and remind her that even preachers' kids, it is said, sometimes get off track for a season. After reading the preceding chapters, I am certain that the reader will agree with me that she went above and beyond what is necessary to give the very best to her children! One thing for which we are very thankful is that none of the children have been wayward in the sense of rebelling against parental authority and deliberately going their own way. We have been spared the many tragic traps into which many youths of today fall victim.

The detours notwithstanding, the institutions that the children have attended over the years include Penn State, University of Maryland Baltimore County, Bowie State, University of Oklahoma, Howard University and Cornell University. At the time of writing this book, Parry was a business analyst at the New York Times, and Kwasi was hired by SpaceNav and is working at NASA Goddard Space Flight Center in Greenbelt, MD, as the Terra Command and Data Handling Engineer. It has been his childhood dream to work for NASA. Bozuma completed her degree from Cornell and is working as Legal Administrator with Faegre Drinker law firm in DC. The baby, Tina, completed her M Ed from Howard University and is an elementary school teacher in Virginia. As at writing, both Kwasi and Bozuma were enrolled in a Certificate in Data Science at Harvard University. There is no denying that Theresa would have loved to have one of her children follow in her footsteps as a doctor. But that is yet to happen. Just like mother, it is not too late yet for that to happen.

While writing this book, I asked Theresa questions every now and then. One time, I asked her to tell me her parenting objectives. She stated that she wants her children to have self-respect and respect for others, especially adults, be trustworthy (sincere and truthful), and hardworking, striving to be the best they can be. It is not important to pursue a glamorous profession; it is important that one pursues excellence in their chosen profession. Lies, white or any other color, are not tolerated at our house. Whereas our family remains strongly bonded and intact, there were times when one parent was away for very long periods of time. In fact, such forced temporary separations have become part of the Acquaah family life.

Chapter 9

A Dream Deferred, A Dream

Realized

n the preceding chapters, I introduced the matter of Theresa's childhood dream of becoming a physician. I shared how she failed to qualify for medical school in Ghana and instead had to settle for a degree in Agricultural Science. Further, I shared how the dream was rekindled in the US but also had a "false start," compelling her to take a detour via MS and PhD degrees, before getting back on track in Oklahoma. This aspect of her life deserves to be told in detail and more completely. It is a powerful and inspiring story of delayed gratification, persistence, perseverance, determination, tenacity, and faith in God.

Upon reuniting in Oklahoma, with our doctoral degrees in hand, we settled into the next phase of our lives. We settled for four children and devoted our attention to raising them the best way we could. We also settled into our first full time professional jobs as university professors at Langston University. I was in the Department of Agriculture and Natural Resources, while Theresa was in the Department of Biology. I had been with the university for about three years before she joined me. With two cars, it was easier for us to juggle our professional roles with attending to the needs of the children without much problem.

Our first single family home in Chowning Heights, Edmond, was located near a daycare center, making it easier for Tina's needs to be met. When we moved to our next house on Buckhorn Drive, the school buses stopped right in front of it. This made it convenient for us in managing the children's school transportation aspect of family life. Of course, we tried as much as possible to get our campus schedules to be favorable to our obligations at home. Edmond was about 35 minutes away from the university. The children came home at different times. By law, children cannot be left by themselves until they attain a certain legal age. Unfortunately, the youngest child, Tina, returned home ahead of the rest. We made every effort for one of us to be at home to welcome her. Unfortunately, despite our best efforts, there was one occasion on which I was about five minutes late. The bus arrived on time and promptly discharged its precious cargo. Tina was not a happy camper when she knocked on the door and no one came out to open it. In fact, normally, we came out immediately we heard the bus arrive. When I finally arrived, there she was, sitting in the driveway facing the street, with head buried in her laps, crying. Thank God, I was only about five minutes late, but that was unnerving for a child. It never happened again, of course. When the boys were much older and could be home by themselves, it was most welcome news for us.

Our second family house was in a prestigious neighborhood of Edmond, Faircloud Hills. It was sandwiched between two golf courses and only about three miles from one of the most prestigious addresses in the Oklahoma City area, Oak Tree, where a couple of PGA tournaments were hosted while we were there. Naturally, the children added golf lessons to their recreational activities. All the children attended Northern Hills Elementary School and Sequoyah Middle School. For high school, they attended Edmond North High, where Parry and Kwasi played in the school marching band and also participated in the Air Force JROTC program. Edmond is a predominantly White neighborhood. One could never miss our children in an annual class photo. For them, this was normal life. They made great friends over the years that they continue to keep.

Living on the affluent side of town had its privileges and challenges. The schools were great. The neighborhood was safe, and

67

they were bent on keeping it that way. We were only one of a handful of Black families in a cluster of neighborhoods in the area. We enjoyed living there and did not experience any major incidences that we could not overlook. Some minor occurrences included children bolting indoors on a couple of occasions as I walked through the neighborhood on my way home. In fact, I once quit in the middle of a fundraising activity organized by parents (boosters) for the school marching band program, when people hung up on me upon hearing my voice on the phone soliciting for donations. One time, while waiting outside the changing room of a local YMCA for Kwasi to come out after a swimming lesson, I heard the voice of a small boy commanding him - "Hurry up, hurry up!" Upon hearing her son's voice, his mother peeked in to inquire from him what the matter was. He replied: "Mom, I am waiting on this Black kid to leave the dressing room so I can change my clothes." Of course, a parent can take anything directed at him or her, but when one's child is involved, that is a different matter altogether. I opened the door, peeked in, and then looked back at the mother, for the child could have only learned that kind of behavior from home. That was the last I saw of them in the gym, at least during the scheduled time for my son's lesson.

Theresa loved teaching and was loved by her students. In fact, she did not hesitate to give motherly advice to students. A case in point is James Wilson, whom she called to her office for a strong admonishing to straighten out and fly right. He heeded the advice. Years later, I bumped into him at a USDA professional meeting in Chicago. He introduced me to the audience by saying, I am here because of his wife, who refused to give up on me in college. Theresa made special effort to make a difference in the lives of minority students, urging them to excel and take advantage of opportunities in the system to be all they could be. Of course, her life story was compelling for anyone to ignore. Notwithstanding her success as a teacher, Theresa felt unfulfilled. The desire to pursue a medical career would just not go away. In fact, it intensified with time. She continued to have recurring dreams of herself in a white coat making rounds on patients in a hospital setting. She was now approaching forty years old. We talked and prayed about it and decided to go for it. Yes, it was time for Theresa to revive her dream of going to medical school. By that time, we had become permanent residents, thereby satisfying a primary requirement for international students for admissions to state medical schools. She contacted the Oklahoma University Health Sciences admission office to find out about the requirements for prospective candidates. Then she requested for her transcripts from the University of Cape Coast, her *alma mater*.

Because the educational system back home differs from what obtains in the US, the course descriptions were not compatible for a one-for-one match, and for direct course substitutions. Further, the grading systems were different. The service of a professional transcript conversion company was required. Their recommendation was that Theresa needed to satisfy the requirements for Physics I and II, Chemistry II and Organic II. Some of these courses, specifically, the physics requirements, had been satisfied in the last two years of high school, called the Sixth Form. Unfortunately, they were not part of Theresa's collegetranscript. She had no choice but to fulfill the requirements, if she wanted to study medicine in the US.

The next challenge was how to take the needed courses, while balancing life as a full time professor and raising four children. Theresa decided to enroll in Chemistry II at her place of work, Langston University. Fortunately for us, we lived very close to the University of Central Oklahoma, in Edmond. She enrolled in Physics II at that campus. For Physics I, Theresa decided to obtain the syllabus from the department, study on her own, and test out. She worked very hard that year to complete all the requirements with excellent grades. It was very challenging, but she persevered. Maybe, this was a test of how she would handle a grueling medical program to come down the line. With the basic courses satisfied, the next step was to prepare for and take the MCAT exam, the proficiency exam required for application to medical school. At that time, the exam comprised of Biological Science, Physical Science, Verbal Reasoning, and Writing Sample.

Theresa enrolled with Kaplan to facilitate her preparation. Rather than attend scheduled classes, she decided to purchase the MCAT package, but prepared on her own to cut down the cost. Her first attempt at the exam yielded only average results. She decided to enroll with Kaplan for the full service the next time. It was during this time that she discovered a major deficiency in her learning style. She found out that she was very slow at reading, causing her not to complete her tests within the allotted times. Theresa consulted with Dr. Lin, an English professor friend and colleague at Langston University, who assisted her with tutorials and materials to improve her reading speed. As indicated in a previous chapter, standardized tests were new to us, coming from an educational system in which exams were mostly essay type. Theresa needed to work hard on her test-taking skills. Most of the weekends were devoted to intense work at the Kaplan center, doing as many practice exams as possible. Her hard work paid off. Her MCAT scores significantly improved at the second attempt.

Apart from course work and MCAT, applicants to medical school need to satisfy additional requirements. Experience with the medical field and some volunteer work are advantageous for success in gaining admission to medical school. Theresa spoke with our primary care physician, Dr. David James of Westbrook Family Practice in Edmond, who allowed her to shadow him periodically on the job. She wanted to have additional medical experience and so she applied to the Edmond Regional Hospital for consideration. Without any formal medical training she had to submit to two weeks of intensive training in order to qualify as a nurse's aide, before she could interact with the hospital staff for the needed experience. Without that training all she could do was run errands. She enjoyed the opportunity so much that she did it for about two years. With all the requirements completed, the next step was to apply to medical school.

Considering the fact that our family was together again after a long separation and our youngest child was only three years old, the choice was not a hard one to make. She decided to apply to the University of Oklahoma Health Sciences Center, that was located only about a twenty five-minute drive from home. This was the only school she applied to, even though she received a recruitment letter from the University of Pittsburg Medical School. Theresa submitted her application in July 1998, just before the family left for Ghana to attend the funeral of her maternal grandmother. Upon return in August 1998, the much awaited letter of invitation for an interview arrived. Three days after the interview, the exciting news of acceptance to the University of Oklahoma Medical School arrived as well. Alas, the dream of becoming a medical doctor was one key step closer to becoming reality. She was about to become a medical student at the ripe age of 40. The offer came with a partial scholarship award. The 2003 class comprised of a cohort of 150 students, six (6) of whom were African Americans, and two of those males.

Admission to medical school was marked by a formal entry event, the White Coat Ceremony, at which the freshman class was introduced and sworn into the medical profession. After reciting the Hippocratic Oath, listening to a number of speeches about the journey of a medical student and professional that lay ahead upon graduation, each student was robed in a white coat. At that moment, Theresa's actual dreams showing her wearing a white coat and making rounds with her friend Dr. Ivy Dankwa Ekem, became reality. In attendance for this special occasion were family members, the Barkohs, from Wichita Falls, Texas, and local friends Blessing Igwe, and Dr. Sarah Thomas, Chairperson of the Department of Biology, Theresa's department at Langston. We had a joyous celebration afterwards at home.

With all the excitement of admission to medical school and the White Coat ceremony out of the way, it was now time to begin the hard work of training to become a doctor. The first two years of the medical school curriculum comprises of preclinical sciences. The courses Theresa took included gross anatomy, cell biology, histology, embryology, human behavior, immunology, microbiology, neuroscience, physiology, biochemistry and medical pharmacology. Theresa had a background in plant sciences and hence had not been introduced to some of these courses, except biochemistry, immunology and microbiology. Consequently, she had to work very hard to successfully complete these foundational courses. She acknowledges that she fully expected medical school to be a very intensive program. Nonetheless, the sheer amount of course work was overwhelming. Add to this the responsibilities of managing a home, taking care of four young children and one can understand how hard Theresa had to work through medical school. I used to be fascinated by the thick textbooks she brought home.

With the voluminous amount of materials to study, her challenge with speed reading soon caught up with her. The class was divided into groups or modules and assigned separate rooms that served as their "homes" in the Basic Science building where class-based course work was held. A module served as an important place for small group discussions, while class mates provided mutual vital support structure and social networking for success. She recalls that one of the students in her module was a little older than her, and had two children. Naturally, the two of them bonded pretty well. She and her colleagues formed study groups to help each other through the hectic program. Students took turns taking notes, printing them, and sharing among members of the group. Being a slow reader, Theresa paid others to take notes when it was her turn to do so. They had "block exams" in medical school. She recalls how she was always among the last students to leave the exam room. After an exam, most students went to Brick Town, a popular part of downtown Oklahoma City, to unwind. However, Theresa did not have the luxury of participating in such social events, instead opting to hurry home to be with her family. She completed the first two years very well.

The evenings at home during the first two years looked like large family study sessions. In spite of her heavy course load, Theresa always made time to guide and assist the children with homework as necessary. I love to write. By the end of the four years of Theresa being in medical school, I had also written and published two new major textbooks. Theresa left home at about

7.00 am and returned around 6.00 pm. She spent some of the weekends at the library. I took over most of the house management roles and chores, both in and outside the house.

In the matter of chores, Theresa and I admit that we failed to train the children to keep to any regimen. We did not enforce cleaning of rooms and making of beds with regularity or a sense of duty. We failed to impart to them the excellent management and cooking skills we learned back in Ghana. Instead, we emphasized studying and doing homework. The children participated in a wide variety of extracurricular activities. Regrettably, there was little significant father and child play time, the traditional kind that builds unique bonding between a parent and a child. In fact, I felt rebuked when Kwasi asked me one day: "Dad, why don't you play with us?" Of course it was not as if we did nothing together at all. We played some indoor games and some basketball every now and then. I guess the children were looking for something special beyond just accompanying them to the many sports and music lessons as well as trips to competitions and recitals.

Towards the end of the second year, Theresa took her first major qualifying exam, the US Medical Licensing Examination (USMLE) Step I, and passed it. With that out of the way, she could proceed to the clinical aspect of the medical school curriculum. The last two years of medical school consisted of planned clinical rotations. Students had to rotate through a combination of required clerkships and electives/sub-internships. This diversity of experiences was designed to assist students in selecting specific areas of medicine in which to concentrate or specialize. The rotations included Internal Medicine, Obstetrics and Gynecology (OB/GYN), Pediatrics, Surgery, Family Medicine, Emergency Medicine, Neurology, Psychiatry, and Rural Medicine. These rotations notwithstanding, many students come to medical school with a preferred area of specialization already in mind. Of course, some change their mind when they are exposed to other options during the rotations. During the rotations, the trainees are expected to manage patients under the direct supervision of medical residents and attending physicians. One may say that this is where the rubber meets the road, and trainees learn and practice the art and science of medicine. They learn by keeping the regular hours that a professional in the area would keep. Theresa recalls that the surgical rotation required longer hours.

73

During the Surgery and Gynecology Oncology rotations, she sometimes started her rounds or patient visitations as early as 4.30 am.

Through assisting with surgical cases, she grew to love that particular area of medicine. The Obstetrics and Gynecology rotation exposed her to the care of pregnant patients, labor and delivery, with a surgical component from gynecology. She pursued a sub-internship in Maternal Female Medicine that involved the management of high risk pregnant patients. Even though Theresa's childhood dream was to specialize in OB/GYN, she started the rotations with an open mind and deliberately reserved the OB/GYN rotation for the last experience. She realized that it could be a stressful area of practice. Nonetheless, the experience only deepened her interest in the area, coupled with her personal obstetrical challenges with childbirth. About halfway through the fourth year, she took and passed the USMLE Part 2 exam.

With this major hurdle out of the way, she began to intensively research various medical programs, their pros and cons, as well as places for medical residency where she'd receive intensive preparation in the program of choice. Theresa wanted to be on the East Coast of the country for various reasons. Family visitors from Ghana always come to the cities on the East, never venturing far into the heartland. When they come, she only gets to visit with them over the phone. More importantly, her younger sister, Josephine, lives in Silver Spring, Maryland. She wanted to be close to her. So, the hospitals she selected for residency were mostly on the East Coast, including programs in Maryland and York, Pennsylvania. But she also included hospitals in Dallas, Texas, and of course the program at her *alma mater*, the University of Oklahoma. Oklahoma was selected for the primary reason of keeping the family together. Following the applications were interviews for these prospective medical residency sites.

Apart from the White Coat ceremony, another event in medical school that is celebrated with fanfare is called the Match Day. It is at this assembly that students learn if their choices of specialization and program site had come true. Theresa and her colleagues gathered at one place to enjoy one last meeting of the graduating class together. At the right time, a sealed envelope with the details of the residency program to which they had matched was handed to each student. When the instruction was given for them to be opened, there was jubilation for those who received their first choice, and mixed emotions for others who had to make do with the less preferred options. Theresa matched with York Hospital, PA. She celebrated with mixed emotions, happy to have matched with a program of her choice, but sad about the impending four years of yet another separation from the family. She was very impressed with Dr. Marian Damewood, the Director of the Residency Program at York Hospital during her interview, and thus was very excited about the match she received.

Before leaving for York, there was one more formal event in medical school to participate in - graduation. This occurred on May 31st, 2003. What a day of rejoicing that was for Theresa and the family. First and most importantly, a lifelong dream that was deferred for about 20 years had now been realized! Thank God!! On another note, that was the first time Theresa was attending any of her graduation events in her higher education life. She missed her BS graduation ceremony in Ghana, and skipped the MS and PhD ones in Michigan. The Doctor of Medicine (MD), was extra special, and nothing was going to keep her away from that event.

To add to the importance of the day, her oldest son, Parry, was also graduating from high school at the same time. Talk about double the pleasure.

As many family members as possible, from far and near who could attend, did so. This included her cousin Sarah Aggrey-Smith and her family from Atlanta, Georgia, our friend Samson Adade from Peoria, Illinois, Blessing Igwe and family, from Edmond, Oklahoma, and Dr. Zola Drain from Langston University. Unfortunately, a family emergency in Ghana compelled Theresa's older sister, Paulina, of London, UK, and Josephine, of Maryland, to miss the glorious event. Her auntie, Elizabeth Barkoh and family of Kerville, Texas, came a week later for a special "make-up" celebration.

The graduation ceremony was a beautiful and memorable affair. Theresa took time to say goodbye to friends and classmates. Then, it was time to get back home for the party. The catering of the party was a "battle" of two exquisite cooks - Mrs. Takyi-Micah and Mrs. Aggrey-Smith. Of course, the dishes were primarily Ghanaian, up to the deserts. We had Fante *kenkey*, fried fish and *shitto*, *jollof* rice, goat meat dishes...just name it. There was music and dancing till late in the evening. Family and friends who could not attend in person sent messages of well wishes via cards and telephone.

After a few days, the visitors had to leave back to Georgia. Then, reality set in; Theresa had to leave for York, PA. This happened two weeks after graduation. The family geared up and travelled along to assist her to settle into her apartment. We stayed with her for a short time. When the time came to separate, again, we said our goodbyes, controlled our emotions as best we could, and departed back to Oklahoma. I had all the children to take care of alone, but Theresa was never far away. She called daily to check on us. She visited about once a month, or whenever possible.

Her apartment was only about 5-10 minutes from York Hospital. Medical Residency is a very grueling experience in the preparation of a physician. The hours can be very long, including day and night work periods. Theresa made a number of very good friends during the period, including Wendy Zeng, Wendy Davis, Carlos and Art. Her apartment was next to a mall, one of her favorite places to visit in her downtime. Whenever possible, she visited it and did what she does best - informed, discriminatory, and savvy comparison shopping. Over the four-year residency period, she was able to shop for a substantial amount of the furniture and household items that we needed for our new house in Gettysburg. She supervised the building of that house. Her apartment became a temporary warehouse, if you will. I flew in from Oklahoma as needed to assist with decision making.

After training, comes finding a job. This is where Dr. Kwadwo Baryeh, a Ghanaian colleague and friend, comes into the picture. He recommended Theresa to the Wellspan Health recruiters, who then contacted her. She subsequently did a four-week rotation with the organization at their Gettysburg Hospital location. After the period, she was hired to join the OB/GYN group that included Dr. Benita Ellsworth, Dr. Charles Mark, and Dr. Kwadwo Baryeh. The office support staff included several Medical Assistants, Liz, Katherine and Pam, in the early years. As at writing, her support staff included Yaritza Salaza and Fabiola Lopez, two outstanding Medical Assistants whom she deeply appreciates.

Chapter 10

Manager Extraordinaire

heresa's life as told thus far indicates a life that is jam-packed with diverse activities that are conducted simultaneously. Is it any wonder therefore that I testify to the fact that she possesses extraordinary managerial acumen? How can one be a great wife, go to graduate and medical schools, work while in school, have and raise children while in school, excel as a student, become a successful professional, and a great mother and wife, and not be a great manager of time and other resources?

Without a doubt, one of Theresa's strongest assets is her exquisite managerial acumen. She likes to plan and plan well ahead. She hates surprises. Part of the reason for this characteristic is that she is highly risk averse. She is a worry bug, and will be in tatters in a hurry at the first mention of adverse news. The irony of this fact is that she likes to know everything! Knowing this, I always try to find the best time to break any adverse news or share certain information with her. The down side to this strategy is that, I don't always do it in a timely fashion, sometimes resulting in her finding out before I've had the chance to tell her, and thus appearing like I was hiding something from her. I have seen her read letters between the mailbox and the house. On the contrary, I can receive a letter and not open it for days.

The fact about people who live tightly planned lives like Theresa is that they function best when life unfolds according to plan. Further, to ensure that life goes according to plan, they like or need to be in charge or in control of events. Theresa is "Mrs. Boss." That sounds unkind. But before one gets the wrong idea, let me say that it is actually a term of endearment. Our family was introduced to the term via a favorite family movie, *Australia*. In it, a young Aborigine boy fondly addresses his adopted mother, "Mrs. Boss." Theresa may be the boss, but she is not bossy. I stumbled on the children one evening as they watched TV in the living room, and overheard one of them make this remark: "We know who is in charge at our house, Mom," apparently in response to a question posed to the TV audience by the host of the program that was in progress. I stuck my head in to help them put things in the proper perspective. As the man of the house, I explained, I will always be the head of the Acquaah family. There is no question about that. Being the head of the household does not mean that, like a dictator, I make all the decisions, and like Jack of all trades, I do everything. We each have strengths and weaknesses. Mom, Theresa, is a better manager and better equipped to run the day- to-day affairs of the family. We need to support her so she can do what she does best, for the benefit of the family.

Theresa really likes to be in charge, but not in a bad way, though. She enjoys calling the shots because of her flare for management and organization, which I accept as far superior to mine. She feels a strong sense of responsibility for her family and wants to be certain that everything is in order. For her worry-bug personality, she needs to be in charge to reduce surprises that cause anxiety. She enjoys taking care of the family. And, truth be told, her decisions are almost always spot on. She thinks far ahead into the future, making preparations and provisions for eventualities. A wife is supposed to be "a helpmeet" for the husband, complementing and completing him. "The two shall become one," is the Biblical admonishing that married couples ignore to the detriment of their marriage. I recognize her qualities and willingly surrender to her lead in those areas in which I am weak, regardless of what the norm may be in society. The truth of the matter is that yielding to her did not always come easy. I had to learn to do that. Theresa is a Suze Orman fan. I am terrible at managing finances. To ensure that her message of financial management is inculcated into the upbringing of our children, and also to help me improve in that area as well, she made watching The Suze Orman Show a family requirement for a season. Whenever we were all together, the TV was tuned to one of the weekend shows of the program, whenever possible. When Parry moved out of the house, he confessed that he watched the program quite often. As soon as they started to work full time, Theresa encouraged the children to implement the financial plans that Suze promotes on her program. Growing up, each of the children had mutual fund accounts established for them at a very early age. We the adults have life insurance policies as well as retirement accounts, in addition to mutual funds.

When the children were young, we celebrated birthdays in the traditional way, inviting their friends of appropriate ages to attend well-planned parties, replete with cake and toys. Now that they are older, birthdays are celebrated by either going out to eat at a restaurant or ordering food for the events at home. Theresa prefers to celebrate with family, the whole gang together. The birthday person gets to choose the restaurant to go to or order from.

Theresa plans for both small and big projects, especially when money is involved. Concerning big-ticket items, such as the purchase of a home, Theresa planned how to pay off our mortgages as soon as possible. I am proud and pleased to say that, as at writing, our primary family home is paid off, thanks to Theresa! The others are not far behind. She facilitates the entry into the workforce of the children by planning to assist them with their first car and place to live. We have been blessed in a special way, as pertains to the places of work and the schools the children attended. When the oldest child, Parry, started work in Maryland, we assisted him to purchase a four-bedroom townhouse. We paid down the price of the house to bring it down to what his salary at that time would qualify him for. It was a very wise move, for it has become a very practical asset for the entire family. It helped him to build up his credit record and also learn some of the responsibilities of homeownership. As at writing, Parry had moved out of the house into an apartment in Virginia, where he resides with his wife, Rebecca. The house has become the second family home, the primary one being in Gettysburg, PA. When Bozuma started work, her first job was in DC. It was very convenient for her to live at that house. As at writing, Kwasi is the only one living in the townhouse. We gather there on special occasions. Also, when I am unable to return home to PA after work at Bowie State University, I have a place to lay my head.

Women are often labeled, unflatteringly, as people who love to shop. To keep us financially sound, Theresa shops very wisely. She is an avid coupon clipper. She identifies items on sale and takes advantage of the opportunity to stock up. Thanks to advances in technology, businesses have access to some personal information that enables them to send people unsubscribed materials loaded with enticing offers. Theresa likes to use her credit cards for even minor purchases. The key thing is that she pays off the bill in full at the end of the month. I believe her buying habits have been carefully analyzed and sold to businesses, and hence she is a target for tons of junk mail. When one is called often by store clerks to remind one of sales, it is clear one is known and loved as a regular customer. Unfortunately for these businesses, Theresa is a very savvy shopper who will not fall for advertising gimmicks. If the price is not right, there will be no buying.

When she goes shopping, she will roam the entire mall searching for sales and deals. A markdown of 50% is not a deal. It must be in the neighborhood of 70% and more to meet her standards. Sometimes, she makes comments like: "I saw a beautiful xyz. The price was too high; I will keep my eye on it and watch for the price to come down." After a couple of markdowns, she might say: "The price is still too high; I will wait a little longer." Sometimes, her wishes come true, other times, she returns home kicking herself for missing that item because she waited a little too long for the price to fall. Her shopping philosophy, if you will, is "buy the best at the lowest possible price." She often argues: "Why pay full price when you can buy an item on sale? Who will know if your shirt was purchased on sale or at full price, unless you tell people?" It is fair to say Theresa is a "sales expert" of sort. She never met a sale she did not like. When I can, I sometimes wiggle out of going shopping with her. One of the first sentences in Akan, our native tongue, that our children learned translates into "Let's go, let's go [home]." After about an hour at the mall, I've had about all I can take. On the other hand, that's when the real shopping begins for Theresa.

What sets Theresa apart from the traditional "shopaholics" is that she shops with other people in mind more often than for herself. She is not one of the women with a shoe mall at home; clothing, may be. It is not uncommon for her to come home with two pairs of shoes, half a dozen shirts, a couple of pants, and accessories just for me alone. On a good shopping trip, our house looks like a mini mall – tons of stuff for everyone. Another very important fact about Theresa's shopping habits that must be pointed out is that she has discriminating taste. Nothing but the top of the line, whether clothing, accessories, furniture, groceries, just name it, will do. She goes for the highest quality at the lowest price. So, don't pass judgment when she passes by, decked out in brand name items, and think this lady is extravagant. She is not a high maintenance woman. She is very high class at affordable price. That said, every now and then, even Theresa indulges in high-priced items.

She stocks the freezer with freezable food items when they come on sale – BOGO (buy one get one free). I don't see her use coupons any more, but she certainly reads store flyers and takes note of sales. In Edmond, she found out that a grocery store near our neighborhood marked down all roasted chicken products by 50% at about an hour or two before closing time. She changed her shopping schedule to evenings so she could take advantage of the sale. Sometimes, I must admit, I feel a little uncomfortable when she gets into the haggling mode with salespersons at the mall. "Can you reduce the price a little?" "What sales do you have today?" "Will the price come down later?" Come on, babe, pay and let us go home. When I go shopping by myself, not only do I come off at the wrong end of the bargain quite often, but I have to answer to her back home: "You mean you paid $xxx for this?" "Did you ask for a reduction in price or you just paid what was advertised?" "What is this? You call this nice?" So, to avoid catching all this grief, I simply let her do the shopping. She always buys the best, anyway.

Theresa continues to shop for the family. The challenge is that, as the children grow older and become more independent, they want to buy their own clothes and develop their own identities. Unfortunately, sometimes, Mother does not understand why a nice dress is not appreciated by the recipient. "Where is the coat I bought for you?", she might ask. Of course, it is in the closet or under the bed somewhere, because he or she does not like it that much. On the other side of the coin, it can be a pain, sometimes, to buy anything for Theresa, especially, on a special occasion like her birthday or Valentine's Day. The first question always is "How much did it cost?" Come on, can't you just say thank you and leave it at that? Sometimes she might add: "I know you want to show appreciation and love, but you know we don't have money at this time." Or, she might say: "Don't buy me any present. We don't have money." Sometimes, I just go ahead anyway to buy her stuff, the traditionally safe bets for presents, like flowers on Valentine's Day, and nice items when I travel overseas. Just because she would rather I not buy her presents, does not mean she detests them all together. She gets upset when I forget a special day – birthday, anniversary, etc. On our 30th Wedding Anniversary, I accompanied her on a shopping trip and asked her to pick an item for a present. This way, I knew that both the price and the taste were right.

Theresa is very practical. "Why buy a present for $50 for Christmas when you know that it will be on sale for $25 or less just a day after the event?" she might say. For adults, this is a reasonable argument; but for children, it is not. So, when the children were younger, we got them gifts for the occasion, but waited for the sales that followed the event to buy other stuff. When we moved into our family house in Gettysburg in 2008, between the stored items in her apartment and what we had at our Edmond home, we had enough brand new furniture for the entire house. She recalls that, one time, a colleague wondered why she was doing all that buying. "Theresa, you will soon be an attending physician and have all the money you need, so why worry yourself now?" her friend asked. Well, Theresa has a large family both in the US and back in Ghana to support, medical school loans to pay, as well educational loans for the children to pay. She has no choice but to use her resources wisely.

Effective time management skill was critical in enabling Theresa to juggle school work, parenting and professional life. It was critical to be on time for classes to be successful in college. And when she worked, it was even more critical to keep a schedule that permitted her to arrive at the job site on time after school. It was also important to keep the schedule for daycare, to avoid paying extra for overtime. The schedules grew more complex as children were added to the family and school activities, regular and afterschool, were factored in. By the time we had four children, we literally had no time for ourselves. When a trip overseas was to be undertaken, Theresa scoured the Internet and locked in the best prices as soon as possible. She took advantage of the off season sales to accumulate presents for family and friends back home.

Theresa is a multi-tasker. She approaches life with urgency and purpose. I will let her colleagues opine on the quality of her work, but there is no doubt in my mind, from the little I can glean from a distance, that she is committed to her work and strives for excellence on the job. When on call, she pays undivided attention to her patients, and is eager to stay at the hospital rather than be at home, so she can provide immediate help as needed. She has never skipped work because she wanted to have fun with family.

One cannot live in America for long before hearing about the so-called "American Dream." How did that factor into our planning? The idea that anyone can succeed through hard work and playing by the rules appears to be at the core of this noble concept. However, it appears that the idea keeps changing with time. Currently, it seems to emphasize homeownership and upward mobility in society as signs of prosperity. I don't believe Theresa set out to pursue the American Dream *per se*, however it may be defined. Rather, she set out to pursue a lifelong dream of becoming a physician, and also to have and raise children who would become successful global citizens. If that is the American Dream, so be it. It turns out that she has achieved the essence of the concept and can even be a poster child for it, as an African immigrant, who has succeeded spectacularly in America. Of course success and prosperity mean different things to different people. For Theresa, amassing material things is not an end in itself. In fact, success and prosperity are meaningless to her, unless they are linked with the success and prosperity of others, especially, the disadvantaged people in the rural areas of Ghana. It is the plight of these people that challenged her to become a physician in the first place. Consequently, she continues to work her plan to someday set up a medical facility to serve her community in Ghana.

I have shared candidly about our family and especially Theresa in this chapter and others, because I know she is very confident and secure in herself and does not mind me doing this. She is not pretentious but authentic and transparent. What a woman! I hope someone will be inspired by her lifestyle and emulate it.

Chapter 11

Celebrating 30 Years of

Marriage

As Christians, we took our wedding vows in accordance with biblical teaching. According to our belief, God unites couples. Divorce is not an option, unless under extraordinary circumstances. Marriages are made in heaven, it is said, but are lived on earth. The implication is that the honeymoon, sooner or later, gives way to the realities of life. I have heard about the expression "itchy seven", implying that after seven years of marriage, the tensions in a marriage reach a level where divorce is often considered.

Well, by God's grace, we've made it for more than thirty years, 37 to be exact as at the time of writing, and we intend to continue till death do us part. We'll share more on this later. We never celebrated our 25th wedding anniversary, a more special milestone than the 30th in my opinion. July 30th 2013, was our 30th wedding anniversary. I wanted to do something special for this special anniversary. I started planning very late (men!). I wanted to keep it a surprise. I wanted to take Theresa to one of the Caribbean Islands for a romantic week. True to form, she would not take time off from her work for fun. This time, I was to blame, totally. She had used up her two-week vacation earlier on in the summer. If only I had communicated my intentions to her sooner, she would have saved those days for our special get away.

I settled for something local. Following the recommendation of one of my colleagues at work, I booked a couple of days at the Poconos Cove Haven Resort in PA, for a quick romantic getaway. It turned out to be a great getaway. In consultation with some lady friends of mine at work, I selected an exquisite set of jewelry fit for an anniversary gift. This time, I decided to run it by her first. For that kind of money, I did not want to risk getting her something she would not like. It was a wise decision, for she stated emphatically that she was leery about buying jewelry online. She was right, for when we ended up visiting her favorite jewelry shop at the mall, we picked up items that we both loved. As a bonus, I ended up getting an exquisite anniversary wedding band, to replace my 30-year-old original band, which was tight and choking my finger. In fact, Theresa had insisted that I discontinue wearing it until we got it resized. I declined her suggestion and kept it on to avoid feeding the rumor mill, if you know what I mean.

So, what transpired over 30 years of marriage? Were expectations met? What worked and what did not? Just like the Oprah letter, I wrote Theresa an anniversary letter as follows:

Wedding Anniversary Wishes

To My (Almost) Perfect Wife

Today, July 30, 2014, marks our 31st wedding anniversary! On this wonderful occasion, I thank God for giving you to me. I am truly the most blessed among men, to have you. There is none perfect, except God. But you, my dear, are "My (almost) perfect wife," the title of an authorized autobiography of you that I am currently working on. My prayer is that the Almighty God would fit it into His plan to grant us another 30 years of marriage bliss, filled with great health, prosperity, and love that passes all understanding!

Our first 30 years together have been great, no doubt. Ours has been a very unique journey, to say the least. For what is supposed to be a "union," we have spent about half the time leaving apart, physically! We started off with a "forced separation" only a week after our wedding, because I had to leave for the US! It would be at least a year before we would be re-united. After my doctoral program, I left for Oklahoma for about 3yrs before we were reunited under one roof. Then, after your MD program, you left for Pennsylvania for about 4 years, before we came together again. Now, it looks like "living together apart" is our lifestyle, for you work in Pennsylvania while I work in Maryland. We see each other usually on weekends.

By God's grace, what would have torn others apart has kept us together and going stronger!! We shall grow stronger and stronger with time, for as long we do not lose sight of the fact the marriage is first about us. We must continue to make each other our first priority, and make time for and celebrate each other, especially, considering our peculiar circumstances. Above all, we must always remember that God is the third and indispensable party in our union.

Over the years, we have been blessed with four very wonderful children! We continue to advance professionally. We are healthy, even though we've had various major health challenges in recent years. We've had our fair share of marital "friendly hostilities," not unlike all marriages. It was all part of growing pains, two lives being transformed to become one, in a constantly changing world! Hind sight is 20/20. Looking back, some things were just silly mistakes that could have been avoided. We cannot change or live in the past. Leaving the past behind, we must press on.

On this anniversary day, I want to let you to know that there is no one I look forward to sharing the next 30 years with more than you! We have made it work for the last 31 years; we know how to make it work for better. I am thankful to God and deeply appreciate your exquisite qualities superb organizational and planning skills, excellent financial management acumen, love for and dedication to family, professionalism, God-fearing, trustworthiness, faithfulness, etc. Please rest assured that I am only too happy to yield to your leadership in areas in which you are superior! My only regret is that I did not yield sooner. I want what is best for you and the family.

I appreciate your sacrificial devotion to me and the wellbeing of the family. Like your mother of blessed memory, you are always *willing to go the extra mile for the sake of the family. The kids and I may not have always expressed or said it enough, but we are no good without you!*

So, sweetheart, it is with unalloyed joy that I write this letter to thank you, profusely, for who and what you are, my (almost) perfect wife.

Love, always.

George

Some information must be corrected in the letter, as was done in the Oprah letter. I decided to change the title of the book from *"My (almost) Perfect Wife"* to its current title, because we both taught something different would be more appropriate. Change, it is said, is the only constant in life. Everything changes with time. So, how have Theresa and I changed over the past thirty years? As scientists, we know there are many agents of change in nature. Similarly, there are many agents of change in a marriage. Some factors of change are common to all humans; others are unique to the couple. To form an alloy, two metals must be melted together. To become one, sometimes a couple must go through fire, so to speak. Fire has a way of burning out impurities and leaving the metal refined and pure. Similarly, in order for a marriage to thrive, certain aspects of the union must literally be "burned out." This could be attitudes, habits, or other factors that are unhelpful to the union. I-centeredness must give way to We-centeredness, in order for a more perfect union to occur.

Every married couple hopes to live happily ever after the wedding. Unfortunately, change happens, relentlessly, and then hopes may be dashed. Like it or not, everyone ages progressively. With ageing, hopefully, one becomes wiser. Unfortunately, change is so unpredictable in its specifics. No one can predict how one would age. In addition to individuals changing separately, the couple must change together. This is where the rubber meets the road, so to speak. This is where a major challenge lies in a marriage. Ideally, the couple should complement each other, one being stronger where the other is weak. With time, there may be the need to reshuffle roles in a marriage. One may have to yield to another in areas where the other is superior. Traditional roles of men and women may be reversed as needed to make the marriage work under a specific circumstance.

As if that is not complex enough, the society in which we live itself changes unpredictably. The natural environment is constantly changing. There are human-engineered changes that may be positive or negative in their impact on society. Politics impacts all we do in society. Administrations come and go, following their agendas, and achieving different outcomes. The economy may do well for a season and take a turn for the worse later. The American Dream may be more challenging to realize as the economy sputters. The couple may experience bouts with major health issues, sending their plans suddenly into a tailspin. A couple may plan to have children and then down the line realize a medical challenge would make it impossible. On the other hand, one may be blessed with children and then find they may not progress according to expectation or even go wayward. This is but a small sample of change factors a couple may confront during a marriage. Of course, some changes would be positive and perhaps more than the couple expected. The way they succeed depends on how they handle the inevitable change. Some people are reactive, while others like Theresa are proactive because they plan and prepare ahead. Some people have no "shock absorbers" to handle the bumps along the way of life; others are able to use various resources, such as faith in God, to weather the storms that may come.

A lot can happen in thirty years to a person. With time, the spirit can grow stronger, but the flesh, unfortunately, tends to grow weaker and start to manifest wear and tear, as it yields to the laws of nature. For example, attempts to cover grey hairs are successful only for a short time, that is if one can keep up with the biweekly regimen of dyeing it. The waistline is often a challenge for both men and women to keep in check. Four pregnancies and an equal number of children can take their toll on the tummy. Theresa has over the years tried to get rid of the so-called "baby fat" with mixed success. Spandex can only do so much good to tighten and keep rebellious body parts in check. Sooner or later, gravity compels body parts that once stood at attention and pointed right into the viewer's eyes with defiant firmness, to now point downwards, with drooping embarrassment. Not to worry. Modern society has an "Apps" for nearly everything. The vagaries of age notwithstanding, I often catch myself stealing a glance at my wife and saying to myself: "After all these years, she has still got it!" After all these years, Theresa is still a very beautiful young lady, completely natural, no nips and tucks.

Much more than just anatomical changes have occurred in our bodies over the past thirty years. We have matured as human beings, emotionally, spiritually, intellectually, and socially. We have learned to put off childish ways in our actions including speaking, thinking, and reasoning. We are older and certainly wiser. We have developed and advanced professionally. More importantly, her dream of becoming a physician, though delayed, materialized twenty years later, when she received an MD from the University of Oklahoma. Thank God!! America is a land of opportunity. If you apply yourself and work hard, you can achieve great things and live comfortably. In fact, there is no way we could have accomplished such outstanding professional success, if we were back in Ghana. Our children have also achieved outstanding success in their endeavors.

Thirty years is a very long time to be together. We've had some light moments of laughter and joy. We've had some anxious and sad moments as well. The children have given us great moments of joy but also some anxious ones, as we have shared in previous chapters. We lost loved ones over the years, sometimes suddenly and unexpectedly. When these sad events occur while one is thousands of miles away, like being away in America, it can be more challenging than when one is in Ghana. We were able to go home to attend some of the funerals. Since being in the US, Theresa has lost her grandmother, mother, older brother, niece, a couple of aunties, to name a few. Likewise, I lost my father, mother, my older brother, a couple of uncles, cousins, aunties, among others.

On the health front, Theresa and I have had some challenging times. During the final year of my doctoral program in 1985, I was involved in a head-on collision accident while on the way to my research site. The car was totaled, but thank God, I escaped with only minor injuries. After that, Theresa was diagnosed with hyper-parathyroid tumor condition that was linked to the premature birth of our second son. She also had skirmishes of her own with her car at various times, but without serious injuries, just like me.

In the later years, Theresa and I have experienced major health challenges. First, she had a cardiac episode for which she was receiving treatment. She was diagnosed with a 98% blockage in one of the critical arteries to her heart, the so-called "widow maker". A stent was placed in to correct the problem. Not long after that, it was my turn to scare the family. I was diagnosed with prostate cancer. Thank God, it was caught at stage two; the cancer had not metastasized. I received appropriate treatment. We are both doing very well. It is important to mention also that these health issues, deaths, and other challenges sometimes occurred simultaneously or within a short span of time. One of the kids was involved in horrific accidents a couple of times, but thankfully escaped with only minor injuries. As they say, when it rains, it pours.

In terms of living arrangements, our marriage has been very peculiar. Couples marry so they can live together. In our case, it appears we married only to live apart! When couples live together, they can benefit from immediate help and support from one another. Theresa's accomplishments are more amazing considering these long separations that compelled her to be saddled with the load of running the house all by herself for several years. When joined in the east coast, we chose to make Gettysburg our home city, so Theresa could satisfy the emergency response time of her medical practice. This is about a two-hour drive to my workplace in Maryland. After one year of exhausting daily commuting, we decided that I stay at our Silver Spring townhouse during the weekdays, and come to Pennsylvania on Fridays for the weekend. We have been living this way for the past 12 years. Thanks to COVID 19 and the attendant lockdowns and school closures, we are enjoying our longest stretch of time living under one roof! We pray and hope that the pandemic will be brought under control swiftly, though.

Theresa is very protective of her family. She is mild mannered, but not a pushover. She will stand for her rights and defend her interests, in major and minor situations. For example, when she goes shopping, she reads her receipts with a fine-toothed comb to ensure that she is not cheated. Some stores advertise one price and charge another at the counter. She'll demand any error be corrected. She'll hold the store accountable for a rain check. However, Theresa knows when to let some things just slide, for indeed, some things are not worth fighting over.

During the COVID-19, as she continued to serve dutifully at the frontline, she experienced her first direct insult of the racial kind. As she walked from the parking lot of the Gettysburg Hospital to her office, one woman rolled down her window and called out "Hey, nigger!" She brushed it off and moved on. Unfortunately, she's had unpleasant experiences that had racial undertones, to which she had to respond. We have always lived in good neighborhoods in the US. These places have been predominantly White neighborhoods. One fateful evening, in Oklahoma, Theresa had stopped by a gas station to fill up her tank. She paid at the pump. Tina wanted a drink, so she went into the store to fill up a cup at the soda fountain and proceeded to pay for it at the counter. As she exited the store, the manager followed and confronted her with an allegation that a customer said she saw her shoplift candy and place it in her purse. Naturally, she did not take it well and let the store manager have it! In fact, she was so upset that she called the police to report the incidence when she arrived at the house. It was unfortunate that one of her children, at an early age, had to witness her mother being falsely accused and humiliated that way. This incidence occurred when Theresa was at a critical time during her medical school program. Imagine how stressful it was for her to endure this experience.

Another store incidence involved two of our children. They had accompanied their mother to the neighborhood grocery store. She had given each money to purchase packs of soft drinks. As theyexited the store, the manager followed them to the parking lot and demanded to see the receipt for the purchases. Of course, Mother Theresa demanded to know why that was necessary. Similarly, just like the gas station incident, a police car just pulled into the parking lot just about the same time. Not able to provide a sensible reason for his actions, the manager apologized, and offered to let her have the items free of charge. Theresa rejected the offer.

Frustrations lurk at every corner one turns in life. When people have to live as students, professionals, and parents, simultaneously, there are numerous sources of frustration to ruin each day. The day at the workplace may not go well, through no fault of the couple's. The traffic back home may be jammed to Timbuktu. One may arrive home, finally, only to be greeted at the door with yet another home-made challenge. What comes naturally is to react and transfer all the pent up frustrations to whomever is at the door, one's spouse or child. Consequently, instead of coming home to wind down, one comes home only to be wound up some more.

I believe after 37 years of great marriage, I am more than qualified to give advice on the subject. I share about our life together, sincerely, to let the reader know that we are not exempt from any of the challenges that confront married couples. Through it all, by God's grace, we have overcome many adversities. It makes Theresa's life and accomplishments even the more amazing. I've said before that she is an ordinary woman who continues to live an extraordinary life. What does not "kill" her, makes her stronger. In our case, we had another layer of challenge. We were transplanted from our African culture into a new culture - American. We did not have the benefit of being raised in this culture; we arrived to live our adult life in an alien culture. Theresa was truly "Made in Africa, and Made it in America," the title of this book. One of my favorite quotes, which incidentally was created by me, is: "Strive to succeed (excel), not because of, but in spite of." In other words, one should not let one's circumstance be an excuse for doing nothing and feeling sorry for one's self. As Christians, we live by the biblical dictum: "I can do all things through Christ who strengthens me." Nothing just happens! God is able to work all things, good and evil, for our good. His plans are for our good, not evil.

Once an African, always an African. After thirty-seven years in America and counting, Theresa has not forgotten from whence she came. She remains very proud of her native country and people. We love America and thank God for the opportunity to live and serve Him in this country. In this era of globalization, we are ambassadors of Ghana to America, and *vice versa*. We are agents of collaboration and partnerships for the mutual benefit of our two countries. God bless, America, and God bless Ghana!

Chapter 12

The Kids in Their Own Words

ne of the desired blessings in life for a married couple is to have children. Theresa and I are blessed with the best children a husband and wife can hope for – Parry, Kwasi, Bozuma and

Tina (Ernestina). We are blessed to have two boys and two girls. They were all born in America, unlike their parents who are naturalized citizens, having immigrated from Ghana, West Africa. For Theresa, family comes first. There is nothing she likes more than having her family together, not only on special occasions, but whenever possible. She sacrifices so that the family can have a comfortable life, lacking nothing. One of her favorite things to do is cook for the family, something she does often even when she is sick. Theresa is devoted to her children and puts them ahead of herself.

Now, staring at an empty nest, and contemplating retirement as at the time of writing, Lion Mom is not yet ready to completely cut loose the pride. She often cooks and sends the delicacies to their homes in Silver Spring, DC and Virginia. She buys presents for each one at Christmas time. She continues the family tradition of dining out on birthdays, at the birthday person's restaurant of choice. This is a very popular outing the kids cherish so much. She still shops for clothes for them, albeit not as much as before. She is gradually accepting the fact that they are now independent adults who have developed their unique lifestyles.

Thus far, I have shared how we, as parents, feel about the kids and how I feel about their mom, Theresa. I have described some circumstances in our family life over the years that were stressful. But how did the kids really feel during those times? I have shared how we bent over backwards, in our opinion, to provide what we thought was best for them, but was that really what they wanted? I indicated that Theresa sometimes even second-guessed herself, and wondered what if she had done certain things differently, specifically, not pursuing her dream of becoming a physician? But should she blame herself in any way? Then is the pink elephant in the room, the long separations between parents, and especially between parents and the kids. How did that affect them, if at all? Because the kids are a huge part of Theresa's life, this autobiography will not be complete without hearing from them, in their own words. So, I interviewed them for this chapter, and provided an opportunity for each one to contribute a paragraph or two about their mom that would be included in the book, unedited. Among other things, I asked them to recall some funny moments as well as not so fun times. I have shared these sentiments in the detail that I deem appropriate. We have opened a window into our family life, with the hope that our experiences will be helpful to other parents. Much as I believe Theresa is a superb wife and mother, no one is perfect, and hindsight is 20/20.

To help put the kids' sentiments in proper perspective, it is important for the reader to be reminded that two distinctly different cultures are at play in this story, African and American. Theresa was a young woman, aged 26, when she arrived in America. She was by then steeped in the Ghanaian culture, born and bred in Africa. The way children are raised in Ghana is significantly different from how it is done in America. In our case, the differences were magnified by the fact that, even though there are people of color in America, the neighborhoods we have lived in to date have always been predominantly White. Growing up, the kids knew only America, their birth place, and nothing about Africa, their parent's land of birth. Naturally, they saw differences between the family life of their White friends and that of their African home, and also learned from what was portrayed on TV, at school, or when they visited with friends. If even we had wanted to adopt and adapt to the traditions of our new environment, it would not have occurred overnight. Further and more importantly, we would have examined the new culture critically to see what was worth emulating and what was not. Consequently, it should be expected that we would have started doing what we knew to be best for us, first, before incorporating new ideas later into our lifestyle as necessary.

Let me start this general discussion with the matter of communication – verbal, physical and emotional. Strict discipline is part of the general training regimen of children in Africa. You don't get to take a time out for throwing a tantrum; you might get spanked. Children are spoken to often in tones that are authoritative, giving instructions that are to be obeyed rather than negotiated. Often, children do not mix with adults at a gathering, unless invited to do so. Your parents are not your buddies or playmates. Display of affection, especially intimate ones like kissing, even among adults, is uncommon especially in public. But in America, the opposite of what I have described appears to be the norm. Naturally, kids in African homes in America might observe the disparity and wonder what could be wrong with their family.

The reader would recall I mentioned earlier that one of the kids asked me one time, "Dad, why don't you play with us?"

In Ghana, and I believe most countries in Africa and developing countries in general, very few in society have the opportunity to live the "good life." Consequently, parents usually want their children to grow up to pursue glamourous careers, the 'big ones' as I call them. There are lawyers, physicians, accountants, engineers, businessmen/women, and then there are all others. If you are smart, you must consider becoming a doctor, first. I recall in my days, one of my friends had applied to the Agricultural Science program at university. Then the WAEC results came in, and showed that he had outstanding grades. Immediately, the family instructed him to change his application to medical school. Well, now he is a medical doctor. With this mentality, kids with artistic and athletic talents are not encouraged to pursue these possible career paths. In a way, you cannot blame the parents, for it is their experience that it is hard to make a living in those career paths.

When Africans, and I believe immigrants in general, come to

America, the land of opportunity, the mentality is that failure is not an option. They want to make the most of the opportunities available or create their own. In our enthusiasm to encourage kids to challenge themselves and excel in school, there is no doubt in my mind that we sometimes overlook their natural talents and abilities. After being in higher education for over 30 years, I believe that good education is not about shoving knowledge down the hutch, but rather priming the pump, so to speak, and drawing out what is already in the student, first. Then you can mold the individual into a confident and competent professional, who loves what they do. I believe we can sometimes overdo the example thing. "Did you see this young lady from the ghetto who worked hard and went to Harvard and became a doctor?", we might draw kids' attention to, and with the intention to encourage them to work hard in school. But too much of this approach can be misconstrued by a kid to mean the target for them is ivy league and medical school. They are praised and supported enthusiastically when they lean in that direction. But maybe they want to excel at something else they really like. Afraid to voice their opinion and possibly disappoint their parents, some kids just play along. In the process, they harbor resentment toward the parents and internalize ill feelings that manifest in all manner of emotional behaviors. A quiet child may be harboring deep emotional feelings and yearning for attention and understanding from parents.

As parents, we always say that we love our kids equally, but they know better. It is not uncommon for one of them to feel that they are the black sheep of the family, and that another is favored. Birth order makes a difference to some degree, as experts say, in how children feel in their family. The oldest child tends to be pampered, and so is the last born. Poor middle child! Another critical factor that parents ignore to the detriment of their parenting efforts is that, like the five fingers on a hand, they are all different. Some are late-bloomers, while others start off running at an early age. Similarly, some maintain a steady progression in growth and development, while others take a detour in life before hitting the target. Common statements that kids detest include: "Why can't you be like your brother or sister?" "If this were Paul, he would have done it …". "Did you see uncle Sam's daughter? She is so respectful and hardworking." A frustrated parent can unload on the kids, or worse still chastise one of them behind their back to their siblings. And in the performance area, kids who come home with As are praised to the highest heaven, making their average- performing siblings feel they are less valued. High achievers are the pride of the family who get introduced and paraded in front of guests. "What about me? Are you not proud of me?" the others might feel. In response, some kids will then try to work harder to please their parents. Then what happens if their effort appears inadequate or unnoticed by their parents? Some kids are even terrified to try, because they may fail in a failure-is-not-an-option environment. They are only comfortable sharing their successes, but hide their failures from their parents, for as long as possible.

I am certain some of what I have discussed thus far was the experience of some of our kids in some form. Now older and wiser, they look back and put things in proper perspective and understand. Over the years, they have expressed their love and appreciation for their mom through traditional ways like giving her presents, cards, phone calls and visiting. As I write this book, I am exceedingly proud to give them the opportunity to bring closing remarks to this autobiography about their mother, and more importantly in their own words. The truth is that Theresa made every effort to love the kids equally, but she'd be the first to admit that she may have missed some things, or could have done some things much differently and better. That said, if the testimonials of the kids below are any indication, she did good, really good!

Parry is the oldest of the Acquaah bunch. He was a natural born talker, like mom. He was a very curious child, who asked a lot of questions about anything. He became an information junkie at a very early age. When he learned to read, there was no stopping him. He could walk into the parking lot and identify every vehicle correctly by model and make, without reading the labels. At the airport, doctor's office, or friends' homes, he always reached for the magazine rack or coffee table displays. And yes, he would even pick up the Wall Street journal and proceed to read it from cover to cover. Is it any wonder that, as at writing, he is a business analyst at the New York Times?

Parry did well in school, but had some minor detours in college that gave mom heartburns. Now in his own words:

"Mom is remarkable because she is the true embodiment of the sacrificial spirit. There is nothing she would not do for the ones that she loves. She continually considers the needs of others before thinking of herself, arranging her life to accommodate others. I became aware of this at a very young age. During her time as a doctoral student, she made time for me to explore new activities, try different things and see what I'm passionate about. Her schedule was always demanding, but she consistently made the time to shuttle me to lessons including tennis, swimming and the piano. I didn't turn out to be a professional athlete or a musician, but it did give me an appreciation for music and a desire to succeed and be the best at many arenas of life. There's a little guilt in knowing that she didn't have those opportunities when she grew up. Even at a later age, it didn't seem like she took a deep interest in taking up things like hobbies. Her focus was seemingly always on work, but we all know why that was the case... it was all for us, and for setting us up for potential opportunities and successes in life. I'm happy that because of all her hard work and determination she has accomplished all the things she wanted in life. The inspiration began at home and has always remained with me. There are no words that can express how thankful I am to have her in my life. I love her with all of my heart and hope someday I can measure up to the amazing person she is."

Kwasi, the number two son, had the lowest birthweight, but grew up to be the tallest in the family, now at 6ft 6in, three inches taller than dad. His height was always the topic of conversation in public when he was a child and continues to today. Frankly, I sometimes I get very irritated by strangers and even family folks who see nothing in him beyond his gift of height. "Do you play basketball?", is often what people ask him. Kwasi has embraced his height beautifully, though, and is thriving as an accomplished and handsome young man. Right at a very early age, he was obsessed with anything space. Did I mention that Star Trek is his favorite science fiction? "What do you want to do when you grow up?" we would ask him. "I want to work for NASA," was always his answer. Well, as at writing, he works as Terra Command and Data Handling Engineer at NASA, Goddard, in Greenbelt MD, on contact from SpaceNav. On the hobby side, he is an avid amateur sky-gazer who has captured amazing photos of the world beyond the visible sky. Now in his owns words:

> Mom has always been a person that puts the needs of everyone else before her own. She is the embodiment of showing that hard work pays off in the end. She came to the United States with only 20 dollars in her pocket, she tells us, and started her first job sorting beans as a student research assistant at Michigan State. Now, she's a well-practiced gynecologist that has gained the trust and respect of her patients and colleagues. She has supported me professionally in achieving my goal to work at NASA and I thank her profusely for that. On another note, mom can be a bit opinionated sometimes. Whenever I express a new way to look at things or have her try a game for example, she tends to be cemented in her own ways. She was all work and took life seriously, but sometimes I wish she would loosen up and look at things from other people's perspectives. We have our disagreements from time to time, and I find it hard to persuade her to change her mind. That said, I appreciate all the sacrifices that she made for me that have made me into a person who is passionate about my chosen professional path, and in all that I desire out of life. She encourages us to always strive to pursue progressive excellence. Thank you, mom! I appreciate and love you.

Bozuma is the third child and the older of the two girls. Like Kwasi, she is also a tall young lady. She was always taller than the girls in her class, something that made her a little self-conscious, shy and reserved. She did not share her feelings easily as a child. As she grew older her height, combined with her beauty, made people often inquire if she was considering a modeling career. She was graceful as a shark in the swimming pool, and won numerous swimming awards for her team. Bozuma was an avid reader at an early age, just like Parry. But she was also a good writer at an early age, a skill we failed as parents to nurture. Her teachers thought very highly of her writing starting in elementary school. We encouraged writing as a supporting cast to a career with a more certain future. In college, she was a blogger and even now continues to have a good presence on Instagram. I have decided to encourage and support her to rekindle her dream and take it to new heights. Better late than never. Now in her owns words:

"I wish mom was more openly proud of me. I never really knew how she felt about me or things I had done, bad or good, until months, sometimes years later. I internalized a lot of emotions and sometimes would explode on her. When she was in med school and we sometimes got into verbal fights, I would go for the jugular and say that she wasn't around. I know that even then, she was doing all that for a good reason and for our family, but nonetheless I would be so upset that I would take it out on her.

I have always enjoyed shopping with her; she knows how to get a good deal and has good taste in fashion. I always enjoyed going to the outlet malls or a thrift store with her. Over the years, she has learned what my taste is, and I love everything she has gotten for me. I also look back at some of the photos that I took as a toddler and preteen, and feel lucky to have a fashionable mother. Her money saving habits have robbed off on me.

A funny story that I tell people about how thrifty mom is, occurred when we were in Oklahoma. There was a sale on chicken tenders at the grocery store, but the limit was 3 packs per person. She gave each one of us kids enough money to buy 3 packs. We each got our own shopping cart, acted like we weren't together, grabbed the max amount, went to different checkout lines, and bought the chicken. So instead of getting three packs of chicken tenders, we got 18.

We aren't an overtly affectionate family. We don't end every phone call with "I love you." It wasn't until recently that I remember being hugged hello and goodbye whenever I came home to visit. But I know that my parents love me very much nonetheless. How many people can say they have a mother who had four kids, went to med school full time, and any chance they got, attended my swim meet on a Saturday morning? How many people can say they have a mother who performs intensive surgery one day and the next day, would use those same hands and spend hours carefully unraveling knots and braiding my hair, something she has done up until my mid 20s (and still offers to do)? How many people can say that they have a mother who over the course of four years would wake up early in the morning and drive five hours from Pennsylvania to New York to drop their daughter off at college and then drive alone five hours back home in the same day?

Being a mother is probably one of the hardest jobs in the world, add on being an immigrant in a foreign country, that task becomes even harder. The amount of respect I have for Mom cannot be put into words, even though I have tried to do so here. She has made so many sacrifices large and small for our family, some that I have heard about several times, some that I have witnessed firsthand, and some that I will never know about. My parents came to the United States with barely anything, but through constant acts of selflessness throughout the years, I have been given everything and then some. I have learned so many lessons from my mother. She is funny (intentionally and unintentionally), no one knows more about the Royal Family, celebrity gossip, international viral dances, than mom. She is always unfiltered in her opinions and always asks and engages with me with current events. She is also extremely intelligent: you have to be to have three toddlers, be pregnant, and still maintain an almost 4.0 GPA in college. Even though there are times when it hasn't seemed like it, I am eternally grateful for everything mom has done for me and my siblings. It isn't a love that I always felt, but now that I'm older, I know that it has always been there, it has always been unconditional and I am forever thankful for it."

Tina is the baby of the family. This position in the birth order has its advantages and disadvantages. She was the only child to spend time away from the family by herself with another family, her auntie Josephine's, as previously stated. Tina is a talker like her mom, and has a motherly flare as well, always concerned about the wellbeing of others in the family. She is a good organizer. She advocates for her siblings, but they feel she is favored above all - daddy's girl, they say. Tina has an affable personality and made friends easily at school. She attended my institution for her first degree and so came to my office often, as we rode together. My staff would often say, "Tina is cute as a button." Like mom, she has a very discriminating taste. Also, Tina is very forthcoming and will not hesitate to let you know how she feels. Now, in her own words:

"I have a lot of fond memories of my childhood with mom. I recall when she would take time to give me a bath, even after her long days at a night shift on a job. During those baths, she would sing the popular song, "I got you babe" by Sonny and Cher. I loved going to the supermarket with mom. Dining out at Olive Garden after church on Sundays was fun. I loved relaxing and watching movies like Beauty and the Beast and Lion King with her and the family.

There were some sad times in my early childhood, unfortunately. I was sad when she left for Pennsylvania for residency, when I was only eight years old. I missed not having her at my school plays and swim practice. I had pent up anger and pain from such experiences that I often argued and bickered with her during my adolescent years, sometimes saying nasty words I did not mean to her. As I am now an adult and can reflect on how I acted towards her, I realize that my pain and emotions that were never expressed but suppressed in my heart truly affected our relationship in a very negative way. I regret being hard-headed and not understanding what she was doing and giving her the benefit of the doubt. I regret hurting her by my juvenile actions. But I am very thankful that she never gave up on me and loved me just the same. I appreciate the sacrifices she made so I could have a good education, not the least of which were the tutors she hired to assist with my classwork and paying my school fees.

I look forward to a bright future with her and the rest of the family. In fact, I cannot wait to get married in the near future and start a family of my own, and more importantly, raise my children according to her parenting style. I would love to see her play with her grandchildren. I pray for long life for us all and a closer relationship with my mom and the rest of the family.

There is not much that I can say about this remarkable woman, my wife and friend, after what the kids have testified to about her. It is obvious she is adored by the family. We pray for great health and long life for all of us, so we can enjoy many more years together. We love you, mom. You are the best of the best!!.

THE OPRAH LETTER

I have left the errors in the letter to preserve its integrity and my own.

February 6, 2003

Dear Oprah:

NOMINATION OF THERESA ACQUAAH FOR CONSIDERATION FOR A SURPRISE BY THE OPRAH SHOW

ABOUT ME

I am a native of Ghana in West Africa, and currently a US citizen living in Oklahoma. I am a Professor at Langston University. My wife Theresa and I have four kids - 2 boys: Parry, Kwasi, and 2 girls: Bozuma and Tina.

ABOUT THERESA

I propose Theresa to be considered by your show for a surprise in view of her sterling qualities as a wife and mother, and her outstanding accomplishments as I have narrated below. Since being in the US, Theresa has obtained an MS, PhD, and now MD, while raising four beautiful kids. It will be a dream come true for her and the rest of the family to receive such an honor from none other than the most admired and accomplished lady in the world. It will be an inspiration to the women of Africa who watch your program with such religious fervor. Theresa's story exemplifies what many

107

foreign ladies do when they accompany their husbands to the US as "spouses of graduate students." Many take the opportunity to "kill two birds with one stone" by also advancing their academic careers.

NARRATIVE

I started this letter about 4 years ago! I declined to submit it then, for reasons that will become clear shortly. Now, if you would allow me, I want to brag about an extraordinary woman, Theresa,...one that I am privileged and thankful to God to call my wife and best friend. We got married in Ghana on July 29, 1983... I was on the plane bound for the US the next week! It would be at least one year before she would join me in Michigan, where I was studying for my Ph.D. in Plant Breeding and Genetics at Michigan State University.

Theresa's first love has always been to become a medical doctor. She did not obtain admission to the only medical school then in Ghana on her first attempt. Unlike the US where one can go to medical school even after pursuing other careers, gaining access to the Ghana Medical School those days was strictly on a "one strike and you are out!" basis. We hoped she would have opportunities in the US to pursue her dreams. Unfortunately, we realized early, and much to our disappointment, that medical school in the US was restricted to citizens and permanent residents. We decided she should turn to "plan B" and pursue graduate education to broaden her horizon, advance professionally, and increase her market value. She was accepted to pursue an MS in Plant Breeding and Genetics, having acquired a B.Sc. in Agriculture in Ghana.

We wanted kids...four of them. So, we got busy. On Mother's Day, May 9, 1985, she delivered by C-section, our first son, Parry, who had to spend time in intensive care because of premature birth. The second boy, Kwasi, was even much pre-mature (also delivered by C-section), because of problems that were later traced to a tumor in Theresa. Having this second child was also a blessing, for it revealed a hidden tumor in Theresa that could have been missed back home in Ghana where the sophisticated and long arduous process used to detect the tumor certainly are nonexistent. Our son spent weeks in intensive care and months on various medical monitors at home, followed by years of physical therapy and developmental schooling for both kids. Theresa's tumor was successfully removed. She has a scar around her neck that she proudly wears, as she says "as a testimony to God's love".

She successfully completed the MS degree, excelling in the process. As they say, a little learning is dangerous. So, she continued her education, pursuing a PhD in Plant Pathology at Michigan State. I was then a post-doctoral fellow. Because we were planning to return to Ghana after my program, and because we knew we wanted more kids, we thought the best thing to do was to try again. This way, if there were any lingering problems, they would be detected while we were privileged to be in a system with the best health care in the world. We did our part, and were blessed with a third child, a girl, Bozuma, carried to full term and delivered naturally, NOT a single problem!! With each child came the admiration from folks around. "How in the world do you do this, Theresa?" "How do you manage to pursue a PhD and raise three kids?" By this time, the boys were enrolled in various physical and educational intervention programs. Consequently, I requested and received permission from my government for more time to take care of family matters. Alas, I had to find a job to support the family! I found it in distant Oklahoma as an Assistant Professor at a small Historically Black University, Langston University. Now, to leave or not to leave the family behind in Michigan? That was the question that faced us. Theresa did not even blink for a moment. She encouraged me to accept the job offer. She was certain she could handle her doctoral studies, work, and take care of the three kids all by herself! Wow! Her, mother came over for a short period, but she had her own serious medical problems and was not much help...in fact, she added to the complexity of the problems. But we were glad she could also obtain the much-needed medical attention.

Theresa completed her PhD program and joined me in Oklahoma 3 years later! Because of the medical and special educational needs of the boys, the US Immigration granted us permission to stay in the US as permanent residents. Theresa obtained a position at Langston University as an Assistant Professor. She was a superb teacher, caring, and dearly loved by all! Crusading with the renowned Dr. Ben Carson's famous video and books (Think Big, Gifted Hands), she challenged minority students to pursue excellence in education and challenging careers (e.g., Medicine). She shared her life story to encourage students to set goals, sacrifice, and work hard to accomplish their objectives in life. She loved teaching, but she still felt something was missing in her life. Like Whoopi Goldberg said in Sister Act 2 "When you wake up in the morning and all you can think of is to sing, then you were meant to be a singer". Ditto for medicine!

We both continued to teach and render quality service to Dear Langston. We also continued the kid thing and added number 4, a precious girl, Tina, the only Okie among 3 Lakers, in 1995. She was born naturally without any problem...full term. After living in OK for several years, it was clear she qualified to attend medical school. We decided she should go for it! She began preparations and was accepted at the Oklahoma University Health Sciences Center to start medical school in 1999, at the ripe age of 41!! She continued to apply herself creditably and has successfully completed the requirements for graduation. It is with thanks to God and great pride and admiration for a remarkable young lady, my wife and friend, that I announce that she will graduate in May 2003...Theresa Acquaah, MD!! She will pursue a residency in OB/GYN. Isn't is fitting that someone that has had a past of OB problems will be devoting her life to helping women in this area? Another exciting part of the story is that Theresa will be graduating at the same time as our oldest kid, Parry, who is a senior!!! Mother and child... pursuing dreams together, oh how marvelous!

While I am happy for her, I cannot say enough about the SACRIFICES this remarkable lady made to accomplish her goal. She washed dishes in a hotel, worked as a lab assistant on campus, and as an aide in a nursing home. She made absolutely sure the kids were of high priority in our lives. I could never get Theresa to take a break to have fun away from home. "What will I say to myself and people, if something happened to the kids while I was out having fun?' I could never buy her gifts on special occasions. "Please, DON'T. Wait until after the season when they are on sale". As you may imagine, the budget was tight. My visa did not permit me to work. What my scholarship provided was enough for just one. I did not want to break the law by doing anything undercover. She clothed the family splendidly within our means, keeping watch over store sale tag markdowns, until it was down to almost free. She took advantage of freebies, much to the scorn of others who thought she was "cheap". Her car had about 300,000 miles on the odometer, no hubcaps. I felt very bad, watching my wife drive this jalopy to school daily, where students drive posh cars. But Theresa did not mind. Someone came and said to me one day that a worker had remarked that she always wore the same shoes to school. It did not bother her. She did not go to the beauty pallor; she dressed her own hair…as well as the kids'. We rarely dined out…costs too much…save for the kids education!! This is but the tip of the iceberg, in terms of sacrifices she has made and continues to make. She continues to use our family "old reliable van" to school. When people hear we are coming to visit them on the east coast in "the van", they plead with us not come in "that" vehicle. But each time we did, and we came back in one piece. Theresa never keeps reminding me of how God has been faithful in giving us that reliable van! She has sacrificed so much for us that it was my real pleasure to take over the home-operation and become Mr. Mom, to allow her free time to pursue the hectic medical program. Pursing the medical program also indirectly helped me advance my professional career in ways that I'd rather not mention. I want the spotlight to shine 100% on her.

Now, you ask me what I want to do for her? What can I give her for graduation? At least, for once, I want to do something VERY SPECIAL for her… if she will let me. I know what she will definitely need as she starts the hectic residency program. But, I dare not suggest the idea for I know the answer….best to pay cash or near-cash for it….save the money for college fees for our son… we must start paying off her medical school loans (she fears being in debt like crazy). So I really don't know what I can get her. Any ideas?

I did not want so send this letter four years ago because, if you found it suitable for your program and used it, Theresa would have been placed in the spotlight that could have added some pressure to the already hectic medical program. But now it is over! It has ended very well. Thank God! I don't know if this story is good enough for your program. But, whatever you decide, I am very pleased I had the opportunity to brag to someone else, especially someone that I know loves to celebrate life and achievement, about this exceptional woman that I am happy to call my wife, my friend...Theresa Acquaah!!!

I love you, my sweet!!

ABOUT THE AUTHOR

Dr. George Acquaah is the Dean of the College of Arts and Sciences at Bowie State University in Maryland. He holds the PhD in Plant Breeding and Genetics from Michigan State University. He is the author of major college textbooks on horticulture, crop production, and biotechnology, including the critically acclaimed "Plant Genetics and Breeding" by Wiley Blackwell of UK. He is the recipient of the prestigious USDA Award for Excellence in College and University Teaching in Food and Agricultural Sciences, and the Millennium Award for Excellence in Teaching, presented by the White House Initiative on HBCUs in the US.

CPSIA information can be obtained
at www.ICGtesting.com
Printed in the USA
LVHW010919211122
733504LV00004B/85